JAN 2 5 2016
4-28-16(4)

Praise for The Comfort Zone Illusion

"The personal story of Susan Neustrom is as fascinating as it is inspiring. Her amazing journey from earning a GED to a Doctorate is a vivid proof of what individuals can achieve if they dare leave their illusive comfort zone in search of purpose, passion, and personal fulfillment. Susan goes much beyond an account of her story by providing a solid framework of knowledge and tools to help us turn our own journey of discovery from a dream to reality."
Elias Christoforou, Organizational Effectiveness & Change Leader

"Prepare to have Dr. Neustrom's enthusiasm 'caught, not taught.' Action steps are provided toward helping the reader get out of their own way: to maximize their potential by fostering new patterns of behavior that enable success and to no longer find comfort in failure."
Diane E. Ferguson, Retired Sheriff Deputy, US Navy Veteran

The Comfort Zone Illusion

Leaving Your Comfort Zone Is Not
So Hard After All

By Susan Neustrom, Ed.D.

20660 Stevens Creek Blvd., Suite 210
Cupertino, CA 95014

Published by Happy About®, a THiNKaha® imprint
20660 Stevens Creek Blvd., Suite 210, Cupertino, CA 95014
http://happyabout.com

Photo by www.mattferguson.com

First Printing: April 2015
Paperback: 978-1-60005-258-3 (1-60005-258-4)
eBook ISBN: 978-1-60005-259-0 (1-60005-259-2)
Place of Publication: Silicon Valley, California, USA
Library of Congress Number: 2015938359

Trademarks

Warning and Disclaimer

Dedication

To my children,
Lisa and David

Acknowledgments

About a year ago, I was cleaning out my office filing cabinet, sorting through papers, and I stumbled upon a class assignment from my graduate coursework titled, "Ten Things I Must Do Before I Die." The paper was dated 2009 and I could tell I had put much thought into compiling a list of important accomplishments, what I believed would make my life complete. As I reviewed the list, to my surprise, many of the ten items identified as significant way back then had been achieved. My bucket list contained some really great things. For example, earn a doctorate, travel to England, be a keynote speaker, and lead a nonprofit. Check it off, accomplished! Pretty good, I thought, way to go.

Even though I gasped in wonder at how many things I could scratch off my bucket list, the very first item, number one on my list of great things, seemed to just glare at me. Really, my first priority is still left undone. Unbelievable! I did not complete what I felt was the most important thing in my life, an accomplishment that certainly needs to be a scratched off before I die. Number one item on my bucket list: *WRITE A BOOK*. Of course, the desire to write a book was present for some time, much earlier than 2009. However, my confidence, capability, and courage to put words on paper, share my thoughts, and expose my inner feelings never was strong enough to actually write a book. Consequently, of all the great things on my list, "write a book" remained number one just waiting for the right time, the right attitude, and the right people to come into my life so I could finish what I believed was of utmost importance.

At last, because of a few, well, many good friends, colleagues, and acquaintances, I can now put a striking line though the first item on my bucket list. Without their help, support, and encouragement, more than likely, I would still be staring at my list, listening to my inner voice telling me I will never write a book, and feeling a sense of loss for what I could not accomplish. Instead, I am happy, joyful, delighted, excited, and filled with gratitude for my circle of support knowing that this book is the result of their belief in my ability to accomplish a goal, even if it took me a long, long time.

Before I thank everyone, I first want acknowledge my eighth grade teacher, Sister Teresa, for seeing something in me, way back in 1963 that I certainly did not see or couldn't even imagine at thirteen. It was toward the end of the school year and graduation was quickly approaching. One afternoon, Sister was returning graded papers to each student. I was not really paying attention to her because I was daydreaming about summer, the Beatles, and boys, not about my future. When she reached my desk, she stopped, looked me in the eyes, and uttered these words as she handed back my paper, "Someday, you will be a writer." I looked down at my paper: an "A" and a gold star. After that incident, I never gave her premonition even one thought. That is, until recently, when I suddenly realized being an author was my calling, my ambition, and my desire. If I had only listened to the words of wisdom from a very smart lady.

Then again, since I waited so long to write this book, I now have more to share with the world. Of course, without the help and guidance of my book coach, Cathy Fyock, I would still be on Chapter One, hoping the right words spring out on the page. I could never get past perfection, nothing was ever good enough. She directed me to create an editorial board to review my work and provide much needed feedback. This was my first attempt at sharing my work and allowing myself to be vulnerable. My cry for help was not in vain because I quickly established the best editorial board I could ever imagine. Thank you to my dear friend and former colleague, Diane Ferguson, for reading every word, shortening my long, drawn-out sentences and sharing her thoughts throughout the entire manuscript. Spending quality time together offering perspectives about the purpose of the book was not only helpful, but reassuring for me to know my experience can help others. She made me understand that my work has meaning.

For the gift of prose and critical thinking, I want to acknowledge Elias Christoforou, an experienced Human Resource and Marketing director and good friend. His understanding of the content of the book combined with thought-provoking questions and suggestions was valuable in developing a theory- and concept-driven book about leaving your comfort zone and creating action steps for continuous movement from stage to stage. My heartfelt thanks goes to Alison Ooms, Higher Brain facilitator and friend, for her encouragement and positive feedback on helping me to realize that my words, writing this book, really does matter.

Without reservation, I could list numerous occasions where people have asked me about writing a book, and with every request, my desire to become an author grew stronger. I have shared my story with many GED graduates, adult students, educators, and people in career transition. Each time I relate the story, I personally relive the journey, tingle with excitement, and sigh in amazement. Without a doubt, I am so thankful for the opportunity to motivate and inspire others. After writing this book, I will finally remove the very first item on my 2009 bucket list. But in all honesty, I can say, the list will not be any shorter. I just updated my bucket list for 2015, and added "WRITE TWO MORE BOOKS" for items 1 and 2.

Time to get back to writing.

A Message from Happy About®

Thank you for your purchase of this Happy About book. It is available online at: **http://happyabout.info/comfort-zone-illusion.php** or at other online and physical bookstores.

- Please contact us for quantity discounts at **sales@happyabout.info**
- If you want to be informed by email of upcoming Happy About® books, please email **bookupdate@ happyabout.info**

Happy About is interested in you if you are an author who would like to submit a non-fiction book proposal or a corporation that would like to have a book written for you. Please contact us by email at **editorial@happyabout.info** or phone (1-408-257-3000).

Other Happy About books available include:

- Better Software. Faster! http://www.happyabout.com/better-software-faster.php
- 42 Rules for Growing Enterprise Revenue (2nd Edition) http://www.happyabout.com/42rules/growing-enterprise-revenue.php
- Jill Rowley on #SocialSelling http://www.thinkaha.com/books/jill-rowley-on-social-selling/
- 42 Rules for Engaging Members Through Gamification http://www.happyabout.com/42rules/gamification.php
- The Unofficial Whovian Rule Book http://www.thinkaha.com/unofficial-whovian-rule-book/

Contents

Introduction

Your purpose in life is to find your purpose and give your whole heart and soul to it.
—**Gautama Buddha**

The room filled quickly, just as I'd antici-pated. One by one, people began looking around and talking to one another, and as I'd hoped, the front row filled as quickly as the back. Because the audience was com-prised of mostly men and women ranging in age from forty to somewhere in their sixties, I didn't have to ask people to move forward to see the projector screen or hear me talk. The up-front seats were not a problem to fill. Most interestingly, I had presented this topic numerous times for job-seekers, from blue-collar workers to executives, and al-ways drew a crowd. Today's presentation, "Eliminating the Fear of Leaving your Com-fort Zone," was no different. Job-seekers—many of whom had not experienced a job search for a long time—wanted to know how to feel comfortable doing something which gave them no comfort at all. The job search may have come easily to quali-fied candidates a decade ago, but now ev-erything has changed: what made the job search even more challenging is most par-ticipants were considering a career change, and moving from "been there and done that" to discovering a career with deeper purpose and meaning.

They came to my presentation because they wanted to know how to feel good about navigating new experiences that were not familiar and how to identify the perfect fit for their skills and strengths. Most of all, they wanted to be motivated and inspired to follow their passion and not allow fear to put a halt to taking action. With notepads in hand and all eyes fixed on the PowerPoint slide, I asked the participants to describe how they felt when in their comfort zone. Descriptive words began flowing, words such as "stress-free," "relaxed," "confident," "knowledgeable," "secure," "unafraid," "competent," and "happy" were thrown out with high frequency as the participants shared their feelings from the safety of their personal space.

The next question I asked of the participants abruptly changed the tone in the room.

What are you feeling now? It was clear from each participant's expression what they now felt was not comfort; instead, it was discomfort.

Ahh, your comfort zone. What a cozy place to be, a place you never want to leave . . . except if your comfort zone, or your *perception* of a comfort zone, is not really providing comfort. Of course, if you decide it is time to make a change, most people will tell you that you need to leave it; others will remind you that leaving will be painful. The thought of stepping outside your so-called comfort zone is downright frightening. What happens is you stay where you are because, after all, you feel comfortable and seemingly in control. Why venture to the unknown? Besides, to change your life now would mean acquiring new skills, adapting to a new way of operating, and making a few mistakes, at least in the beginning. (Starting to feel uncomfortable already?) And, "What about money, my family, friends?" or, "Well, maybe change is not possible at my age." A million excuses emerge as you rationalize why it is best not to make any radical moves to upset the status quo. After all, it has served you well in the past. Hasn't it?

But consider where you are. What may be driving you to change? Are you bored with your job? Not feeling challenged? Is your life in a rut? Have difficulty getting out of bed in morning? Have low to no energy? Feel like life is passing you by and there is so much more to explore? Maybe your career no longer has meaning or purpose and you daydream often about doing something that *matters*. Of course, you might not really know why you are thinking this way, but something is pushing you to change and you can't seem to shake the feeling. Do any of these motives sound familiar to you? Do you seem to have more questions than answers?

What many people describe as their comfort zone—the routine of living, of doing what you must do, meeting deadlines, working long hours, maintaining a full or overfilled schedule, or multitasking—is really not comfortable at all. Instead, what you feel is discomfort while you wait for the opportunity or the right time to do what you really want, possibly in a few more years, or after the kids are grown, or when you make enough money. Will the time ever come, and what is the right time? Certainly, knowing what to expect, being able to do a job well, and keeping active is reassuring. Comfort is associated with pleasure, relaxation, warmth, and a feeling of contentment. Being in your comfort zone should elicit the same feeling. Is that what you are sensing? Are you really in your comfort zone? Could you be feeling the discomfort of being stuck, confused, uncertain, or unsure of how to make a change to align more fully with who you are, and with your strengths, talents, skills, and passion?

The problem, of course, is that discomfort may be hard to detect at first but subtle clues hint at an imaginable change capable within each of us. A thought, a picture, or a vision of doing something different suddenly appears in your mind. Even crazy, outrageous notions flash in and out of your thoughts: like quitting your job and becoming a rock star, or mountain climber, or artist. (There may be some value in following a wild and outrageous idea, something I'll discuss in later chapters). A distraction, possibly disguised as boredom, occurs. While you might disregard what you feel, episodes of boredom, daydreaming, and lack of energy become more noticeable in your present state. You wonder if there is more, something that brings you happiness, serves a greater purpose, and gives you a rewarding feeling. What you once did is not motivating you any longer. But wait! Great things can happen when the seeds of change find fertile ground and take root. You will blossom.

The Reason for Writing this Book

The reason for writing this book is far different from what I had intended to compose. Writing a self-help book about leaving your comfort zone was not my original plan. I actually wanted to write a book about my story: my life and my accomplishments; a story of comfort, discomfort, and great things. Every time I told my story to different audiences about going from GED to doctorate, the response was always the same: "When will you write your book?" I believed the purpose of sharing my story was so other people would be inspired to pursue grand ideas in their lives despite limitations. Yet inspiration does not equate to action. I recognized without providing a "how-to," including a strategy, an action plan, and execution, your vision and lofty aspiration would quickly dissolve in thin air, and you would probably forget the dream and go back to life as usual. I know this to be true because as inspired as I was when I read books and stories about others who overcame obstacles to succeed, I did not take action until thirty years after I dropped out of high school.

In this book, I share many stories about confusion, uncertainty, fear, and success, because the possibilities are endless once you learn how to get out of the discomfort of being in your comfort zone. Staying in one spot too long can limit your growth, stifle your passion, and build walls around your dreams.

Furthermore, this book opens up portals of breakthrough moments: the moments where you suddenly see yourself through new eyes and golden opportunities now await you. Such breakthroughs are certainly "a-ha moments" and propel you into action. This book is written for anyone who has an itch to make positive changes in life and work, and wants to break down the brick walls of "I can't" standing in the way. Looking beyond the illusions of comfort to the stark reality of discomfort, this book offers practical solutions to eliminate fear and challenge limitations, leading you on a journey of discovery of who you are meant to be, doing work that matters with greater purpose and passion.

Breakthrough Exercises in This Book

Yes, you have to do some homework. Not homework like you remember from your days in school. Instead, consider this fun work. How can you begin a journey of discovery without conducting research about you? No, you do not have to be home to do the exercises (unless you feel so inclined). In fact, I suggest finding a new spot—a creative space, a private, quiet area—to get you away from distractions and encourage reflection, at least in the beginning, outside your imagined comfort zone. Later, you will know the place where you do your best work. Because the breakthrough exercises are designed to build momentum and create movement, each interaction with the itch lessens your fear, breaks down barriers, and gets you one step closer to your goal.

In other words, the breakthrough exercises have a specific purpose. Depending where you are in your journey of discovery, each exercise will shed light on you and encourage deep thought. Some exercises will challenge what you think about yourself, and others will help you focus on what you truly want, not what everyone else wants you to do; additional exercises will reaffirm your strengths and values. What you experience through the breakthrough exercises is a deeper understanding of you, and although each is different, the one commonality is each offers a chance to reveal an "a-ha moment." One of those moments (you might have many and you never know which one) is the turning point, the awakening. Welcome the burst of energy, as it will get you where you want to go.

Years ago, I studied karate—not that I ever aspired to reach master level, compete, or do anything other than learn the art, since I am not a person who likes to exercise. When my health club offered the lessons, I thought it might be a great way to have fun while doing a workout. For three years, I attended weekly sessions, practiced centering my position (well, more sporadically than consistently), concentrating on my movement, and exercising for flexibility. Of course, I never mastered the art of karate, not even getting past the white-belt level. Yet I continued to attend class weekly, despite my total lack of skill, because of the *sensei* who had a genuine passion for the martial art. He would often tell his students (especially those poor-performing students like me) every movement is a learned skill: "I can show you, tell you, and demonstrate the move, and you will not grasp the concept; however, one word, one example, or one metaphor can change everything and suddenly you 'get it.'" How true. While other students caught on to moves at different times, I was often fumbling until one "a-ha" moment when everything suddenly became clear and I could accomplish the move. Breakthrough exercises are similar, so get ready for the moment—it will arrive.

Outcomes

This book takes you on a journey of discovery, beginning with understanding why an "itch" appears, identifying stages of discomfort so you can create habits, short- and long-term goals, and an action plan to get you from where you are to where you are meant to be. Certainly, I would like to offer a money-back guarantee if this book does not change your life dramatically; however, change does not occur by reading a book, attending a class, or engaging in group work. Instead, lifelong change is movement (often slow movement), and what I do offer in this book is my personal "itch" occurrence, my thoughts and feelings, my unbelievable discomfort, and a-ha moments derived from life-changing experiences of being a high-school dropout to earning a doctorate, moving from a career to doing work with a purpose, from coaching people in a variety of situations, and from experts who clearly understand change. My bags are packed, my itinerary is in hand, and the time is now. Let's share the journey and travel together.

As I have said, I can't promise the skies will open, the seas will part, and you will transcend to another world after reading my book. Here is what I can promise: an interesting read, good stories, some laughs, new information shared in a unique way, plenty of thought-provoking concepts, exercises to get you thinking and moving, and, of course, an a-ha moment personalized for you, possibly many. I can guarantee that!

Chapter

1 Got an Itch

There is a time for departure even when there's no certain place to go.
—Tennessee Williams

The day began just like any other day. Pulling into the parking lot at 7:45 a.m., I saw the usual lineup of cars, and I parked in my favorite spot, just a short distance from the building and close enough to see activity inside. I was about to turn off the car when a song came on the radio: "Hotel California" by the Eagles. I loved that song! I couldn't leave now, not yet! Knowing what was about to occur, I now believe that the song was just an excuse to prolong the inevitable. In my fragile, stressed condition, I think any tune would have been my favorite. As I turned off the ignition, I felt odd, like I was coming down with the flu and my body was fighting the bug: my eyes were moist, my throat was dry, and my stomach was queasy. Despite what I was feeling, it was time to head for the door.

To put the day in perspective, I need to point out this was the moment for which I had been waiting for a long, long time. This was the day I'd dreamt about and wished for. I had prepared for this occasion, and I wanted to be ready, yet I dreaded it more than anything I have done in my life. Of course, in the back of my mind, I knew it would come, but somehow I thought I would be happy. Why was I feeling so lousy, then? Trudging into the building, my legs felt almost numb, as if every step was mechanical. Combined with an uncontrollable shiver and red eyes, I am certain I gave the appearance of someone who might have had a few nips before beginning the work day. But I was not thinking about how I looked. I was just thinking about how I was feeling. Why was this happening? Every part of my body was trembling, and I wanted run, hide, do anything else but be here today! I hoped to be strong, confident, and ready to face the world. Instead my thoughts kept racing—what am I doing? Why am I being so selfish and mean to myself? I must have totally lost my mind! Is this what insanity feels like?

Unlocking the door of the bank, I could smell the coffee brewing, ready to wake up the first customers of the day. Music played from a radio to break the silence of an empty lobby. The drive-up tellers were having personal conversations between transactions, and the personal bankers were still downstairs in the break room until the clock struck 8:29 a.m., just in time to open the doors. Oh, the usual routine, a predictable routine that I experienced for a long time that unknowingly provided stability in managing my life, my work, my responsibilities, and my obligations. That routine was me, who I was every day, regardless of my work schedule. Over the course of twenty-two years, I worked especially hard to move up the ranks from an entry-level proof operator to Assistant Vice President, an officer of the bank. Everyone—my family, friends, customers, neighbors—knew me as a banker, an identity that I wore like a badge of honor. Being labeled as a banker made me feel important and respected, even if my circle of influence was small, because I had acquired quite a bit of banking knowledge and expertise. In no small measure, everyone thought I was smart. I liked the feeling all too well.

However, on this day, the routine suddenly seemed to move in slow motion. I became keenly aware of sights, sounds, and people. Every movement I made was mentally noted, and my thoughts were not about what I was doing, but rather about not ever doing any of this again. At any other time, I would have jumped for joy if I could give up my day-to-day routine. But today, I couldn't jump for joy, do a happy dance, or whistle a tune. I just wanted to curl up in a corner and forget everything. I felt like I had given up.

You see, this was my last day. I'd resigned. I'd given my two-week notice. I was ending my twenty-two-year banking career. This was it, done, finished, good-bye. This was supposed to be my break-away decision, a step to help me follow my dream of leading a nonprofit so I could help people reach their full potential. But at that moment, I craved to turn back, stop this crazy notion of leaving, and forget the whole thing. What was I thinking? I'd changed my mind. I was ready to keep my routine, my life, and my work just as it was, even if what I was doing was not particularly satisfying, and most of the time just sucked the life out me. Fear, the scared-to-death fear, took over. I spent the entire day crying and regretting my stupid, untimely decision. I kept thinking maybe it's not too late. I could beg for my job back. It would be worth a try, right? I had not been replaced yet, and since I was well-liked, certainly I would be given a second chance. Suddenly I felt so vulnerable, alone, and hopeless.

Fear of the Unknown—Comfort in the Known

If you've ever had to leave your home of many years, move to a different state or country, end a marriage or a relationship, say goodbye to a dear friend, watch your children go off to college, or go through any experience that has left you with a sense of loss, you probably could relate easily to what I was feeling when I walked away from my job. The loss, even if what you were losing was not ideal and now you might be better off, is overwhelming, to say the least. The act of separating from what is known is not comfortable, especially when the choice to leave is yours. Your emotions tell a different story than your intentions.

For me, leaving was so hard. No, not leaving the job; I don't think it was ever about the job. I was leaving a well-entrenched identity that dictated who I was, how I behaved, and how I connected and communicated with people. I liked the comfort of the repetition of every day. I was confident that I could do my job with my eyes closed—there were no surprises, no challenges. Sameness was my comfort zone, or so I thought. I operated mechanically, hoping someday my life would be different. I tried to prove Einstein wrong with his famous quote about the definition of insanity: when you do the same thing over and over again and expect different results. I'd show him.

Certainly, the decision to leave did not happen suddenly. For several years, I would play out the scenario of departure in my mind, not having the nerve to actually leave. To stop the reoccurring daydream, I would tell myself I was lucky to have a job. Of course, the problem was that I got an itch that would not go away. The itch appeared long before I really understood what was happening. All I knew was I felt like I was destined to do more. I was just doing a job, not what I was passionate about, and my energy and enthusiasm was dwindling. I had spent many years volunteering for nonprofit organizations, working with crisis pregnancies, domestic violence, homelessness, seniors, and transitional housing. I longed to lead an organization that offered support to people and shared my value of equality, happiness, and peace. I really wanted to devote my life to helping people in a much different way than in my current career, but I was stuck, frozen, and incapable of change. The price was too high to pay. Since I worked my way up from an entry-level position to Assistant Vice President, I knew I could not submit my resume for a leadership position in the human service field (to help people improve their quality of life), because I would need to be honest and reveal a long-held secret. I am probably not your typical stereotype, the person who would come to mind when you think about failure, particularly since I climbed the banking ladder so quickly. My secret? I am a high-school dropout. Despite what I expressed to everyone else, my confidence, self-esteem, and positive attitude were quite low. Being a banker, I felt like somebody: I could hide behind the label because no one would ever need to know who I really was. My secret was closely guarded, and I was safe.

The Illusion

Banking was the only career I have ever known and it wasn't even a career I chose. I needed a job that paid more than McDonald's because my daughter was ready for kindergarten and I had to be able to pay her tuition. I knew I could not afford parochial school tuition making $1.70 an hour. Even in 1974, that was a low salary. One afternoon, I walked into the bank, applied for a position, and within a day, I was hired. I even had a choice of jobs: Customer Service or Proof Operator. I wanted to learn something new, so I chose Proof Operator. As the years went by,

I found the job convenient because it was close to home, flexible for my many volunteer activities, and the best part was that I got promoted. I became really comfortable with my duties and working with my peers, staff, and customers . . . that is, until I got the itch and everything began to change. I was no longer content. With each year that passed, I grew more restless to move but never really having the courage to make any changes and take the steps to creating a new life.

So here I was, the final day of being employed as a banker. I was turning my back on a career and a company that defined who I was to my family, friends, colleagues, customers, and more importantly, to *me*. The most puzzling thing about this: it was my decision. I wasn't asked to leave, demoted, or even performing poorly. In fact, I was well-respected in the company, had built great customer relationships, and lead a team of talented employees. On my last day at work, I was baffled. Who is this person who made this decision? I not only stepped out of my comfort zone, I ran out of my comfort zone, locked the door, and threw away the key. Comfort zone, really? Is this why I am now so uncomfortable? In reality, I defined my comfort zone as repetition, a label to identify with, convenience, flexibility, sameness, and no surprises or challenges, risks, or growth. When I really thought about it, I reached a stark conclusion. My comfort zone was an illusion.

Let me repeat this statement in case you find yourself unable to move out of your comfort zone. **The "comfort zone" is an illusion. It is not real.** There was no comfort in my zone, the space my mind occupies. I wanted change, not repetition. I wanted to follow my dream, not enjoy convenience. I wanted to be me, not a banker. I wanted to be passionate about my work, not flexible or merely satisfied. I was not comfortable. There was no comfort in knowing who I was inside was not who I was outside. That feeling I experienced was discomfort: trapped in routine, not developing, or discovering who I am, not working with my strengths and my passion or following my true purpose in life. Over time, I became so conditioned to the discomfort, the feeling of repetitive activity that the mere thought of losing this discomfort was too immense to handle. I felt powerless without discomfort, and clinging to the comfort of routine became my security blanket.

Fear Is a Four-Letter Word (So Is Math)

Because I was always embarrassed about my lack of education, I never shared my secret until the itch became stronger and stronger and presented me with my real dilemma: Do I continue to do what I am doing or take a risk and change my life? How much discomfort would it take for me to leave and create my ideal life? I asked myself these questions often, until the day came to make a decision to follow my calling.

To begin, I took the first step of creating my ideal life by disrupting my discomfort zone in 1998. On a warm summer day in July, I walked into the college instructional center, heading for room 100A. I was a bit early for my five o'clock appointment. Good thing, because my mind raced, my heart beat fast, and I had a knot in the pit of my stomach. I tried to keep positive thoughts in my mind (I can do this, I can, I know I can), but at the same time, my evil gremlin voice would try to shout over my thoughts by saying, "You are a failure, you are never going to be able to do this, who do you think you are?"

After all, my first attempt to take my GED was back in 1977, ten years after I dropped out of high school, but I stopped. I couldn't continue because of the fear of that four-letter word. You may know what I am talking about: MATH! I'd failed math in high school, so what made me think I could do it now? I told myself many times that I didn't need a GED anyway. I'm not smart enough for college, so why bother? But that same voice that encouraged me the first time to attempt to get my GED kept reminding me that I had a vision and a dream to follow, and I could see it and I could feel it, yet I was overcome by fear. I was afraid of failure but what I wanted more was to follow my passion and help people in a much greater capacity to improve their quality of life and reach their full potential.

So here I was, July 8, 1998, Susan Neustrom, forty-eight years old, a dropout, a failure, a self-described underachiever. There was no sign of the confident banker. It had been over thirty years since I'd left school. I was now ready to take the last two GED tests, Test 4 (Literature and Arts) and Test 5 (Mathematics). I was scared, really scared. At that time, I had a choice of how I wanted to take the test: either on paper or on the computer—but no calculator. I chose paper because a #2 pencil was less intimidating than a computer. When I turned in my math test, I was prepared to fail. But I passed! I passed the math test! At that moment, I went from telling myself during all of those years, "Ugh, look at what you did," to, "Yay! LOOK AT WHAT YOU DID!" Earning my GED stopped the flow of negative thoughts, jolted my behavior, and sparked new life. What I believed to be the end of my education was really the beginning of a tremendous journey of discovery of who I was meant to be. Brick walls of "I can't" were tumbling down and I could now get a peek at my vision.

Thereafter, with each degree I earned (two associate degrees, a bachelor's degree, a master's degree, and finally in 2010, a doctorate in education), I learned that the true value of education is not only knowledge gained: education awakens tremendous power to challenge limitations, let hidden strengths emerge, and deepen self-awareness to achieve your highest dreams. At the same time, I learned how to move from working for a living to doing my life's work, a life filled with purpose, passion, and unlimited potential. Breaking away from a twenty-two-year routine, my defining identity, as difficult and painful as it was, became one of the most important steps in leading me toward my life's work. If you feel the itch of "something is missing," or you seem to be stuck in a daydream, longing to follow your calling (even if your calling is not exceptionally clear) after realizing you have been functioning in an illusion called your comfort zone, then get ready to embark on a journey of discovery.

In the coming chapters, I will share my experience, lessons learned, and all the "a-ha" moments that have the power to change your life. But before you continue reading, let me help you decide if you are ready by asking you a few questions.

1. Do you have an itch that will not go away?

2. Are you stuck in a comfort zone illusion?

3. Can you feel the discomfort, yet are not able to move?

4. Are you searching for more meaning, purpose, and passion in your work?

If you answered yes to one or all of these questions and your desire to make great things happen in your life outweighs the desire to remain in your discomfort zone though you are not sure how to begin, this book will offer a map, a guide, and plenty of breakthrough exercises to move you from where you are now to where you want to be.

I have to warn you though . . . hang on, because this will be exciting!

Chapter

2 | Hitting a Brick Wall

The brick walls are not there to keep us out. The brick walls are there to give us a chance to show how badly we want something. Because the brick walls are there to stop the people who don't want it badly enough.
—Randy Pausch

So you have determined you have got the itch . . . now what? Time to move. But wait, something is in your way, and you can't move just yet because your dreams are on hold until the kids are grown, you save more money, you win the lottery, you lose weight. Okay, let's say all of the holds were lifted. Here is what happens next. The timing is not right, you need to finish a project first, you have too many issues to deal with, everyone wants something from you, you must do more research, or spend more time deciding what to do, or hundreds of other excuses—oops, I mean, problems—crop up to justify the delay. No reason to defend yourself because the excuses (a.k.a. problems) are not imagined. You simply can't. Even if one problem is resolved, another problem seems to slip right in its place. This pattern continues indefinitely and time just seems to fly by. Life gets in the way.

Of course, I can easily write about excuses because I used all of them to delay movement. After earning my GED, I envisioned tons of possibilities and thought I was ready to begin moving. By then, a year had passed since my life-changing event, and one evening, I was casually reading the newspaper and stumbled upon something interesting. In the corner of a page, there was ad in black and white. No larger than a postcard, nothing fancy, cute, or clever. But what caught my attention was the caption, "Earn your degree in two years." What! I always thought earning a degree, especially on a part-time basis, even an associate degree, would take roughly five to six years, if you worked consistently and didn't take a break. (Not that I really knew anything about how college works.) When I was a child, our neighbor Bob, who lived across the street from my family, attended night school (that is what college was called in my day when an adult went back to school). Bob was a single guy, lived alone, and was in his forties. I didn't pay much attention to Bob but my mom would comment about how long he was going to night school. Bob eventually graduated and transitioned to teaching. After all those years of schooling, Bob is a shop teacher at a high school: woodworking, to be exact.

So my perception of college, even if I remotely thought I could do it, was that I would need to give up part of my life just to end up with a degree in shop. I could only imagine the time it would take to earn a degree in something of real interest to me. When I spotted the ad that guaranteed it in two years, I wanted to learn more. In 1999, adult education, accelerated education, was just emerging. Colleges became more aware of the shift in the demographics of their student population and realized more and more adults were returning to school for professional development, job advancement, career transition, or to finish their education because at some point, life interfered with completing their degree. The ad was from College of DuPage, promoting the Adult Fast Track where you could earn a degree in management, marketing, or general studies. An orientation to the program was scheduled and I only had to call the number listed to reserve my spot. Of course, I had to hurry because openings were filling fast and the semester was starting soon. I called immediately and made my reservation. Me, in college! I never dreamed it could happen. This was a chance of a lifetime for me.

When I arrived at the orientation, I looked around the crowded room, and was totally taken aback by what I saw. I will admit I was a bit apprehensive walking into the room at first because I assumed it would be filled with young, potential college students. My anxiety lowered tremendously when I scanned the people sitting in the large classroom. They were my people! Old! I was not the youngest (I was forty-nine) but certainly not the oldest. I found an empty seat in the front so I could see and hear every word about the program. My decision to enroll was made the second I realized there were other adults who wanted to continue their education. I felt a true sense of inclusion, like I belonged here.

Tons of information was distributed, the presenters explained the value of earning an associate degree and even displayed a comparison of the salary levels of people with and without degrees. I did not need any more convincing. I was ready to get started, until the Director of the program stood in front of the crowd and discussed the rigor and all of the details not presented in the literature. The Director was a small-statured woman, maybe in her sixties, impeccably dressed, and pretty for her age. I couldn't help but imagine she was probably very attractive in her younger days. She spoke with passion about her struggle to get the program off the ground and her desire to have all students succeed. She then proceeded to outline what it would take to earn a degree in two years. I looked around the room and all eyes were fixed on the director. My anxiety that left me about an hour ago came back in full swing as she stated, "This is a two-year program. There are no breaks. You go to class two years straight, fall, winter, spring, and summer. To complete this rigorous program, courses are combined. You will be working on two courses simultaneously, which means double the homework, and as an accelerated program, each course is five weeks. You meet on campus four hours a week."

Here was the point my heart sank: "To succeed in this program, you have to give up the life you knew and tell your family and friends to put everything on hold. You must devote all of your time to school. No outside activities, no vacations, no major projects, no distractions, *nothing*."

I left, or should I say, I ran out of the orientation because I couldn't do this. College was not for me, especially something as intense as the Adult Fast Track. I was employed full-time, volunteering weekly at a crisis pregnancy center and working as a schoolroom mom, and to top it off, I was planning a major kitchen remodeling project: gutting the entire room and adding new cabinets, floors, walls. That was it—I couldn't enroll now, the time was not right, I had too much to do. For every stipulation that the Director stated, I had an excuse why I couldn't do it. My excuses were real, but the excuses only masked what I was really feeling: fear. I didn't want to admit I was afraid, especially since I felt so great after earning my GED, but fear of failure was there and the brick wall, a big one, stopped me from moving.

Wall of Fear

What are you afraid of? I mean *really* afraid of? I bet you could answer that question easily without even batting an eyelash. "Fear," "phobia," or however you describe what you feel is real. You know your fear, and over the years, you have learned how to avoid any situation that would place you in front of it. If it's any consolation, you are not alone with your fear, by no means. According to StatisticBrain.com[1], ten of the greatest fears are:

1. Public Speaking
2. Death
3. Spiders
4. Darkness
5. High places

6. People (crowds)
7. Flying
8. Closed places
9. Open spaces
10. Lightning

I know I can easily relate to at least five out of those ten fears. I was not surprised by the rankings but what did surprise me is that one fear did not make the list on Statistic Brain or any other site that I researched. What fear? The one of leaving your comfort zone or what you believe to be your comfort zone. Okay, I'll let

---

1 "Fear/Phobia Statistics," Statistic Brain, accessed November 10, 2014, http://www.statisticbrain.com/fear-phobia-statistics/.

public speaking be first, but the next big one should certainly be the one this book is about.

Of course, I should not be concerned by the omission because fear of stepping outside of what is known, of what is not your usual behavior, or what shatters your status quo is not the same as the fear experienced by standing and speaking in front of a crowd of 1,000 (pretending that the audience is in their underwear does not work, trust me) or entering a room filled with black widow spiders. That fear is, well, just *scary*. You avoid it at all costs. Fear of stepping outside of your comfort zone is different because it is not that you either have the fear or you do not have it. This fear does not get you screaming and running for your life, although what you feel does require you to scream every once in a while just to relieve the stress. It screams at you from the inside out. Rather, fear of leaving your comfort zone begins with an itch, a feeling you want to explore new opportunities, that there is a deeper purpose for your work and greater meaning in your life.

However, the reason fear is not really labeled as fear when you embark on your journey of discovery is because the feeling is gradual, but cumulative. It begins with excitement and energy, moves to chaos and uncertainty, and eventually returns to a sense of great satisfaction and enthusiasm. Quite different than, let's say, the fear of flying, when what you feel is consistent every time you think about traveling by airplane.

The itch, the first sign of discomfort I experienced that there has to be more to life, began as a feeling of excitement. I spent quality time daydreaming about my ideal life and work. How could I have known fear lurked within the itch? I was happy, motivated, and energized. In contrast, when I wanted to take action to materialize the daydream, fear became quite apparent, and I was immobile, incapable of even *thinking* I could do anything different than what I knew. Because fear is such a strong emotion and gives an overwhelming sentiment of inadequacy, I resigned myself to the fact that remaining in my comfort zone (really discomfort) was far better than attempting to escape from it and do something new. At least here, I know what to expect, and I am willing to accept more of the same.

After all, daydreaming is safe and only requires your imagination; on the other hand, taking action is risky, requires commitment, and there is no guarantee of success. So it's understandable that an element of fear would rear its ugly head just when you are ready to make your move. It's always present and your body has its own defense system that works to keep you safe. You know the feeling and you know how you respond.

Conversely, fear during times of change is not the same feeling as all other fears because it is disguised as logic, rationale, and being realistic and responsible. The conversations you have with yourself: you know, the one when your inner voice tells you—no, *demands*—what you are thinking is crazy, so just get back to what you know. Because your inner voice gets louder and louder when you think about change, you are now convinced that to change anything, let alone a life change, is simply not going to happen . . . ever.

Uninspired by Change

The thought of change is inspiring, but the act of change, deciding to put your plans into action, can quickly become uninspiring, leaving an open playground for your inner voice to whisper words of fear. It's a simple fact: change creates fear, but it is not your fault. External forces are everywhere and come from multiple sources. Whether you are exploring options, dabbling in discovery or working on making some significant changes, everyone you encounter will give you advice just to be helpful or to give you a word of caution so you do not fail. Their advice probably sounds like this: "Just let go of the ledge, get over the fear, it is sink or swim." Or how about this motivational quote? Do you feel inspired?

> *Move out of your comfort zone. You can only grow if you are willing to feel awkward and uncomfortable when you try something new.*
> —**Brian Tracy**

I don't know about you, but I don't want to jump out of an airplane without a parachute, walk on a tightrope without a safety net, or swim the ocean without my floaters. Forget it, I am not changing if it means I am going to experience pain, intense fear, agony, and uncertainty. It is far easier to give myself permission to cave into my fears.

Fear Generators

Change, as well as your perceived definition of change, creates five distinct fears. Whether you experience each fear at different intervals, or they all creep up at once, the overwhelming feeling becomes a wall that puts a halt to moving forward with your vision. To determine which fears are holding you back, consider what you are thinking as you attempt to make any change. The five fears are:

1) Fear of the Unknown

WHAT YOU'RE THINKING: I can't see what is ahead and I feel like I'm not in control anymore.

This is the first fear to poke its head out when you think about change. It will probably surface rather quickly, and if left unattended, stop you dead in your tracks.

To get a feel of this fear, imagine it is a beautiful, sunny, warm summer day. You have nothing on your schedule this afternoon, so while driving in your red convertible sports car (with the top down, of course) you spot a road leading into the forest. You've passed this road often but never took the time to explore the route. Today, for some reason, you make a sharp turn onto the mystery path. As you drive, the scenery is breathtaking: trees are swaying in the breeze, a pond with an amazing waterfall is splashing on the rocks, birds are singing, and you feel fantastic. As you are taking in all of the wonders of this path, the road begins to wind but you don't mind because you're the only car on the one-lane road, and this feels so good, you accelerate just a bit more.

Oops! A bump, then you just miss a pothole, suddenly you realize you are driving on dirt, and to top it off, a thick fog begins to roll in and the skies turn dark purple. The comfort and joy you experienced on this road has now changed to stress, anxiety, and apprehension. You tighten your grip on the steering wheel, turn off the radio, and try to squint to see. The road continues to wind, the bumps get harder and harder, and your vision is so distorted from the fog you're certain you are headed for disaster. You want to turn around, go back to the beautiful place you first experienced when you set out on your adventure. But you can't even see the road, let alone turn around, and besides, you made so many twists and turns along the way, there is no guarantee you would end up where you began. Your heart is pounding, your throat is dry, your eyes are strained, and you have to admit you are really scared. To be continued . . .

I will return to this story later, but you should have a good feel of this first fear as you leave what is known and embark on a journey of unknown.

2) *Fear of Failure*

WHAT YOU'RE THINKING: I don't know if I have what it takes to do this and I don't want to hear, "I told you so."

This fear is a surefire wall because no one wants to fail—everyone wants to succeed. Even with the best-designed strategy and action plan, there is no guarantee of success in work or in life. Failure can happen for many reasons beyond your control. Your inner voice really likes this fear, and continues to remind you how incompetent you are, taking control of your life. Don't worry, though, your inner voice will not abandon you with the fear of failure. In fact, your inner voice will be present 24/7 as it intensifies.

3) Fear of Abandonment

WHAT YOU'RE THINKING: It took me so long to build my reputation and career, now I have to start all over again. No!

This one is the no-can't-do-that, can't-afford-to-change, I-worked-too-hard-to-start-all-over fear. When I wanted to pursue a degree in Human Services to transition from banking to a helping profession, my advisor warned me that toward the end my coursework, I would need to leave my banking job and pursue an internship in the field. This fear engulfed me and held on so tight I thought I was going to cry. What! I'm not ready to leave my job, I can't leave everything I know and run off and start from scratch. My fear was so intense, I did not pursue the degree I really wanted.

To put this fear into perspective and not make it seem so terrible, think about buying a home. You looked forever and finally found your dream home, and now you're so excited to move. The first thing you need to do is pack everything from your current house. You suddenly realize it's time to part with the old sofa, the one on which you watched movies with your best friend, slept on when you had a long day, and covered with a sheet so the dog could nap. This is hard. Then there are dishes that are mismatched, and clothes that have not left your closet in years, and the list goes on. You can't take everything so you need to discard items that no longer have a specific purpose. But some items, like your photos, your jewelry collection, your golf clubs, your most precious things, will make the move with you. Of course, you have already made a list of new things you will buy, because after all, this is your dream home and you want everything to be perfect. You move with the things you cherish, discard the stuff that's outlived its usefulness, and buy new, color-coordinated items to make your dream home beautiful, comfortable, and all yours. Similarly, you abandon what you no longer need and what does not fit in your life anymore. Identify what actually gives you comfort from what simply holds you back and weighs you down.

4) Fear of What Others Will Think

WHAT YOU'RE THINKING: *Everyone will think I'm crazy, talk about me, and I risk losing relationships with family, friends, and peers.*

The longer you have been in your career, and depending on your role, the easier this fear can grab hold of you, put you in handcuffs, lock you in a prison cell, and throw away the key, because you care what others think. In other words, it creates the most stress because not everyone wants to see you change and they will make the fact known. They like you the way you are, so why do you want to do something different? The more you care about how others perceive you, and whether or not they approve of your changes, the more intense this fear can become. Your change, identity, and your new behavior have an impact on your closest relationships, so it stands to reason you will meet some resistance and need to make some hard choices about the value of maintaining relationships that create conflict and disruption. Of course, don't be surprised if these changes strengthen relationships in ways you did not foresee.

5) Fear of Success

WHAT YOU'RE THINKING: *I'm not ready, I feel like an imposter, and I'm going to be found out and exposed.*

This is tricky because you will be in denial about ever experiencing it. It closely resembles the fear of failure because of the stalling techniques of not really taking action. The difference between fear of failure and of success is failure fear does not allow action, while the success fear encourages action. To be more precise, fear of success occurs when you do take action, move forward, opportunities are abundant, and the future looks bright. How can fear be present? When you venture into new territory, especially if your journey led you to working in a new field or line of work, you find you need to build up your confidence level in your new role and when things, even really good things, happen, you become afraid you do not have all of the answers, may not be able to make a good decision, and covertly slow the progression of success until you feel ready. You are not thinking about failing, you are thinking about functioning in a new role and identifying with the role. Until you do, you might need to play the imposter role, and if success is chasing you, holding it back through fear becomes your strategy.

> Procrastination is the fear of success. People procrastinate because they are afraid of the success that they know will result if they move ahead now. Because success is heavy, carries a responsibility with it, it is much easier to procrastinate and on the "someday I'll" philosophy.
> **—Denis Waitley**

You need to give yourself permission to be afraid, but not permission to slow success.

Breaking the Wall

Fear, one or all five, is the first response your body experiences when the itch that began as curiosity has now changed to intense discomfort. You can no longer ignore what you want to do. You know your limitations from what you've done in the past but you don't know what you can do. The reason fear is present is because of your perceived limitations of your ability to change what you know you can do. The limitations, your deep-down fears, are the result of past failures, inexperience, or being told you can't do that. Excuses are bricks, and little by little, each brick stacked higher and higher becomes a wall limiting movement, creativity, self-confidence, and most of all, your *vision*. Over time, the wall suffocates your desire and capacity to grow. Surprisingly though, your wall can be toppled by using the right approach to see beyond the limitation.

The first approach to breaking down the wall, brick by brick, is to delve deep into what you really want. Because your vision— your goal—is not strong enough, the wall continues to be a nuisance and interferes with change. Change without a strong motivating force is painful, tedious, and uninspiring. Very seldom is it lasting.

The second approach to chipping away at the wall is to begin taking action, *any* action (however small) because action is a powerful force that can push you to opportunities you never believed possible. Whether you realize it or not, you are always in control but instead of allowing circumstances to dictate your level of control, create action steps that put you in the driver's seat, moving on "full speed ahead." That is, shift your attention away from your weakness, what you think you cannot do, to focusing on your strengths, what you can do. You will notice a significant difference in your thinking because you are not being controlled by your fears, and new strengths develop to meet even the most difficult challenges.

Now that you have identified how fear can build walls to limit your freedom to move, it's time to break down those walls and make great things happen.

Breakthrough Exercise 1

To get started, redefine the perceived definition of change from "feeling awkward and uncomfortable" to "*change is moving from who you thought you should be to who you are meant to be.*" There: does that definition of change create fear?

Now it is your turn to define change, as only you can describe what will happen as you begin movement.

Fill in the Blank

Change is _____

_____

_____

_____

_____

_____

Once you create a personal definition for change that is not aligned with fear, post the definition in strategic places so that you will be able to read it often. Think about putting it on your bathroom mirror, your computer, the refrigerator, your car dashboard, or anywhere you can see it at all times. Record the definition on your phone so you can play it back and hear it in your own voice. Play the recording often.

Your wall of fear might be ten feet tall and made of thick concrete or just a flimsy wall of cardboard. Either way, the wall stops you from forging forward. Next, even though you may not be certain how the wall came to be, try to visualize it.

Go ahead: be creative. Draw your wall just as you envision it because it's holding you back.

- What does the wall look like?

- Is it made of dark, drab brick, or is a newly constructed wall? It's yours and only you can see it.

- As you imagine the wall, what is written there? Here's another opportunity to expand on your imagination. If you ever wanted to experiment with graffiti, now is your chance. Probably want to shy away from spray paint, but magic markers will work.

- What are the words you can read?

- Look very closely: are you surprised at what is written?

- If the wall were removed, what would you see?

You now have designed two powerful forces: a personal definition of change and a very interesting and artistic display of your wall with a peek of what is on the other side.

You are just getting started. Keep going, and feel the wall begin to crack and the dust start to fly.

3 The Worst Advice Ever Given

We delight in the beauty of the butterfly, but rarely admit the changes it has gone through to achieve that beauty.
—Maya Angelou

When you become fully aware of the itch and decide you want to make some significant changes in your life, you will most likely be given advice from family, friends, colleagues, and even total strangers who want to see you succeed but maybe not necessarily want to see you change. Everyone will have an opinion to share about what you should do, how you should or should not do it, and what you can expect to occur—there will be no shortage of advice. Before you become overwhelmed with what to do, consider that advice as something you accept because you never know when a few phrases, a bold statement, or a motivating story will become life-changing words. With all advice, the best approach is to temporarily put it on a shelf with other advice given and decide later if there is any value in following one or all. Certainly, of all the advice you will get, at some point you will probably hear, "Never give up," from people who support you and want to help you achieve your goals. However, even though persistence, despite obstacles and failure, often results in unbelievable success, one thing you should know is that the worst advice ever given may actually be NEVER GIVE UP!

A Noble Value

As a rule, I don't watch television, mostly because I am just too busy, and I find most programs to be boring and repetitive. But for some reason, on a Saturday afternoon in between vacuuming and dusting, I was drawn to a program about emergency rooms. The daily routine of the medical staff working in an environment of high stress, making life-saving decisions, showing care and compassion, fascinated me. In one episode, an emergency room doctor continued to administer treatment to a cardiac arrest patient for over forty-five minutes. Even though the medical team was exhausted, the doctor did not want to give up. Afterward, she shared her life experience of losing both parents to heart disease and understanding the devastating impact on a family when the loss is so sudden and unexpected. What led her to continue treatment beyond a reasonable time was that she did not want to break the news to the patient's family that she'd failed to save his life. Finally, wet with perspiration, breathing heavily, and emotionally drained, the doctor stopped all lifesaving procedures, and announced the patient's time of death. In that very moment, something miraculous happened: the patient had a slight pulse and . . . well, then I went back to my Saturday ritual of cleaning, hoping my doctor would hold the same mindset to never give up if the need ever arose. Certainly, to never give up is a value reaping great benefits. Or so I believed.

Outdated Habits

Seeing that from a very early age, I was always told that if I made a commitment to do something, I must stay true to my commitment from beginning to end, I could never give myself an option to reconsider because I am not a quitter. I told myself those words over and over again. My inner voice would whisper—no, *shout*, "No one likes a quitter. Only a loser gives up." Needless to say, knowing I could not quit made me think twice about what responsibilities I wanted to have on a long-term basis in my life. Of course, holding a strong value of commitment, I probably judged everyone's behavior from my perspective. Well, not probably: most certainly, I made judgment statements about quitters. Maybe you have observed people who give up in the workplace. You know, the employee who just walks out, or in school, the student who drops the course after the first class, or in sports, after a team loss, the player who throws down his helmet and walks away. Of course, everyone knows "never giving up" is a true testament of character and the secret to success. Consider that winners never give up, high achievers never give up, and champions never give up. Because I was so fearful of giving up and held true to a "never give up" mindset, I stayed at jobs even when they were not a good fit, remained in bad relationships because I couldn't bear the thought of acknowledging failure, and continued to engage in habits that were unproductive and energy drainers, to say the least.

Then again, to never give up is such a noble quality, associated with success, achievement, and recognition. In contrast, the belief about giving up is such a disgraceful act, linked to guilt, low self-esteem, and an untrustworthy character. That is why giving up may be so difficult for many people because success requires perseverance and tenacity; therefore, giving up is the same as failing and who intentionally wants to fail?

The reason we struggle with the definition of never giving up is because of our mental model. What our mind perceives as reality is learned through experience. For this reason, to never give up is such bad advice because if you have been conditioned to believe never giving up is positive behavior and giving up is negative behavior, the ability to give up habits, thoughts, and actions that have worn out their usefulness is a struggle and downright painful. As a result of this type of thinking, I continued to hang on to what was no longer working even if my thinking worked against achieving my goals, because of my association with the negative definition.

Quitting Is the New Normal

After all, think about all of the famous people who practiced a "never give up" attitude. Walt Disney was rejected over and over because he was told that he lacked creativity. Thomas Edison and Albert Einstein did poorly in school and were labeled as stupid. Michael Jordan did not make his basketball team in high school. Certainly, these people never gave up . . . or did they?

Success occurs when you understand what needs to be stopped, changed, or eliminated so you can pursue your vision. Steve Jobs understood what it meant to give up.

> For the past thirty-three years, I have looked in the mirror every morning and asked myself: "If today were the last day of my life, would I want to do what I am about to do today?" And whenever the answer has been no for too many days in a row, I know I need to change something.

For Steve Jobs, the question defined his actions until his last day.

If you are stuck in the "never give up" mental model, perhaps there is some anxiety (maybe even quite a bit of anxiety) about giving up anything regardless of the approach, relationships, or habits that are not working. Under those circumstances, giving up is probably not a first, second, or even a third option. In my experience, the act of letting go of the pieces of the past that had no room in the present or future was a huge obstacle hindering movement toward my vision. Giving up, as bad as this may initially sound, is really the first essential step of the transformational change process. By reframing the purpose of giving up from what you will lose to what you will gain gives your mental model a knee jerk. At the same time, you formulate a new thought pattern leading to the discovery of hidden strengths and unlimited potential. Until you purge the encumbrances, there is no room for the potential to emerge and thrive.

Therefore, "never give up" may not always be the best advice because the phrase connects deeply with our mental model of success and failure. Instead, a better approach to success is to embrace your dreams, values, and people who support you, and sweep away the cobwebs, tangles, and debris holding you back from reaching your full potential and becoming who you are meant to be. Better advice?

Breakthrough Exercise 2

If you are still hesitant to "give up," here is an exercise to help you let go. On a sheet of paper, draw two vertical lines, one down the middle and one on the left side of the paper to form the three columns. Label the first column, "Aspects of Your Life." You can add as many as you like. Be very detailed in your list and include all essential, important aspects of your life. Next, think about what you are doing now in your current situation with each aspect. Make that the title of the second column. Then, in the last column, consider what you would really like to do in each aspect. Be bold, don't hold back, and imagine how each aspect could align with your ideal life.

Aspects of Your Life	What I am Doing Now (Current Actions)	Really Want to Do (Future Dreams)
Work		
Relationships		
Family		
Leisure		
Spiritual		
Ongoing Personal Development		

Look at the columns, side by side. Do you see aspects of your life which remain the same in what you are doing now and what you really want to do? How about differences: more, less, same?

As you review your comparison, reflect on the following questions:

- Like Steve Jobs, how many times would you need to answer "no" to change something?

- What could you give up today in order to achieve your goal?

- What must you let go of in order to move toward your vision?

- What are you holding onto that has outlived its usefulness?

- What is holding you back from what you are doing now to what you really want to do?

Keep going, and before long, you can erase that middle column!

4 Does This Vision Make My "But" Look Too Big?

The ultimate measure of a man is not where he stands in moments of comfort, but where he stands at times of challenge and discovery.
—**Martin Luther King, Jr.**

If the idea of change, even the slightest departure from your status quo, is intimidating, you may have resigned long ago to the fact that doing work you love and enjoying an ideal lifestyle is never going to happen. The best you can hope for is to be a financially secure and settle for a relaxed, safe retirement. Of course, the rationale is that you pride yourself on being practical, realistic, and honest, but the truth is, your dreams remain a memory of what could have been.

With this in mind, think about a time when you believed in your vision and who you were meant to be. Your vision beamed you to the future, and your vision challenged you to greatness. With high energy and exuberant enthusiasm, you set your sights on reaching your goal and nothing could stop you. The finish line was just at the end of a rainbow and you *saw* it. But then something happened. You took a hard look at reality and realized your present state was nowhere near your visionary state. As you counted the number of obstacles you would need to tackle first, energy faded, enthusiasm dwindled, and the vision was just too far out of reach.

What's the next thing you did? If you're like me, you probably decided to dummy down your vision; a nice comfortable little vision is much easier to achieve. Of course, you can always justify your choice by adding more and more obstacles to your long list of "But I can't do it because . . ." You come up with so many excuses. That way it is not really your fault for not transforming your big vision to reality.

As an illustration, one of my earliest recollections of a big vision occurred when I was five years old. More than anything else, I wanted to be a cowgirl. I would imagine myself riding a golden Palomino with a flowing white mane, jumping over tumbleweeds and prancing next to a cool stream. It was also the same year I was scheduled to have a tonsillectomy. Every kid in kindergarten was having a tonsillectomy so I was really happy to be admitted to the hospital, and it was not the reward of ice cream after the surgery that excited me—instead, I was totally joyful about the reward of a pair of red cowgirl boots (thus, my love of shoes was formed at an early age). I truly believed I was getting closer to my vision by wearing the red cowgirl boots everywhere.

As I got older, my cowgirl vision seemed to move further and further away because obstacles kept mounting. I would tell myself, "But I don't own a horse, but I have never ridden a horse, but I don't live in the West, but I can't . . ." I felt my vision was hopeless, just a dream. Without knowing, I was developing a pattern for goal sabotage that would follow me for many years.

However, consider the time spent dreaming about an incredible vision that motivates the spirit, awakens the senses, and makes you feel *alive*. The problem with most visions is they are hidden behind walls of obstacles and limitations, and will never see the light of day to flourish into the real thing. Surprisingly, it doesn't have to be this way if a simple technique called Mental Contrasting is considered when you set your mind to reaching your goal.

Here is how Mental Contrasting works. Your vision must have two pictures: one picture is you at the finish line achieving your goal, and the second picture is all of the obstacles standing in your way to cloud your view of the finish line—rocks, walls, chains, curves, potholes, and anything that creates a barrier. In order to achieve your goal, the reality of the obstacles that stand in your way are contrasted to your big, lofty goal. The contrast helps you understand what you must tackle to achieve your goal. By mentally preparing yourself for pursuing it, the path from vision to reality is not a surprise. Instead, you have a clear picture of each obstacle and an even clearer picture of you living your vision. Your focus is on the finish line, "I can do it." Acknowledge the work involved in getting to where you want to be. Surprisingly, the right combination of vision and obstacles is a strong motivating force.

In fact, Gabriele Oettingen, PhD, professor of psychology and researcher at New York University, conducted extensive research on motivation and goal achievement. In her book, *Rethinking Positive Thinking: Inside the New Science of Motivation (Penguin Group, 2014)*, she describes two approaches to mental contrasting. One approach encourages motivation for goal achievement and the other approach discourages motivation for goal achievement. Oettingen discovered that people who understood the difficulties and challenges to achieving their vision and felt optimistic about reaching their goal were more successful than the people who understood the difficulties and challenges to achieving their vision but considered their ability to achieve their vision as low. That is, if present reality, where you are now, consumes your thoughts, the path to your vision will be rocky, treacherous, and steep. Maintaining a steady thought pattern of obstacles is not very conducive to motivation. Similarly, if you continue to daydream about your vision without any consideration about what it will take to transform your dream to reality, time will pass and the vision will never move beyond an escape from reality. The secret to applying mental contrasting is not choosing one single approach, but balancing your approach.

To put it another way, like work and leisure, the key to a healthy lifestyle is balance; therefore, goal attainment is no different. When mental contrasting is considered, challenges become steps to action, small successes become motivation drivers, and your time is spent moving in a positive direction toward your vision. The size of your vision is not important. What is important is that your big, lofty vision is balanced between a high perception of success and obstacles that create bumps in the road to goal achievement. To keep you steady when obstacles appear, consider acquiring a token object to focus upon, a symbol of your vision. Your personal red cowgirl boots.

Go ahead! Now is the best time to dream big, *really* big, because you deserve to live your vision, enjoy your life, and be happy. In fact, recently I have been thinking more and more about revisiting my cowgirl vision. More than likely, I will begin by slipping on my red cowgirl boots.

Breakthrough Exercise 3

There are multiple exercises available for applying mental contrasting, but finding what works for you is the best way to develop a winning formula for goal achievement and making great things happen in your life. Here are two.

1. Vision is a really big exercise.

First, you need to ask yourself two questions to test your readiness to begin a strategy for leaving your discomfort zone.

1. Why is my vision important?

2. What is the driving force compelling me toward the vision?

If you are able to honestly answer the two questions and feel energized and excited, then you have a high potential for success. Using mental contrasting will help you create an effective action plan for transforming your vision.

2. Conduct a vision feasibility study.

- Write down all the challenges you must address to achieve your goal.

- Determine what challenges can be addressed and which cannot change.

- Now focus on the expected outcome (visualize where you want to be).

- Measure the amount of time it will take to achieve your goal.

- Review your study and determine what will need to change (adjustment in your vision or adjustment in your challenges).

When you compare and contrast the challenges to the steps toward the vision, you readily see how to adjust what can be accomplished to what needs to change or be eliminated or redesigned. Your strategy for success is aligned with what can be (future you) and with reality (present you). This technique works and helped me develop a balanced, practical approach to designing my life around multiple visions.

How can you expect a successful outcome even when the vision makes your "but" look so big? As a result of your personal vision feasibility study, you realize the amount of work involved in achieving your goal, and you are in control of your actions and thoughts. Keep going and don't let anyone tell you that your vision makes your "but" look too big.

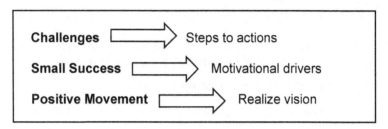

5 Transform Fear into Energy

Everything you've ever wanted is on the other side of fear.
—George Addair

For most of my life, I've lived in fear and didn't even know it. My behavior was me, who I was. Growing up in the 1950s, I grew accustomed to the label that gave me permission to be me, not an imposter. While others believed something was wrong with me, my mother would come to my rescue and forgive my behavior by stating, "Oh, she is just being shy." In school, I would never raise my hand in class, and when called upon, my voice was a mere whisper. At recess, while the other kids were playing red rover or jump rope, I would stand by the school entrance waiting to go back to the comfort of my desk, my personal space, my safe zone.

Certainly, confirming and naming my behavior masked the fear I felt every time I found myself in a situation that created discomfort—a situation where I would be expected to talk and interact in a group. Of course, without a doubt, someone would make a snide remark about my shyness: "Oh, you have to stop talking so much," or, "What's the matter, cat got your tongue?" and the degrading comment would make me clam up for good. Instead of responding positively, remarks about my shyness intensified my fear to speak to anyone.

Eventually, to my surprise, I learned through personality assessments that I was an introvert. Not some of the time, not only in certain situations, but an all-of-the-time, 100% introvert. The fact I was a full-fledged introvert explained why I was shy. I felt worse knowing that who I was then was not who I wanted to be. At that point, I felt trapped because I didn't like being called an introvert. I didn't like the label "shy." I didn't like not being able to think of anything to say to people. I didn't like that I could not speak up in a group. I didn't like that I had very few friends and very limited job opportunities. I wanted to change everything about me. I wanted to be an extrovert and maybe then my life would be different. Can you hear me stomping my feet and pouting?

As I recall, when I was twenty-one, after spending some time contemplating life and where I was going, I declared I wanted to be somebody, not certain who somebody might be, but certain I wanted to be somebody. Of course, being an introvert was probably not the way. Because my perception of success was dependent upon being someone else, not me, I was always frustrated at my behavior. I spent much of my career mimicking behavior of people who were not like me. How did that work out? Well, you can only play a character role for so long until the real you, who you truly are, wants a turn to come out and play, too. It is at this time fear gets into the act and builds a wall to keep both of you apart. Nevertheless, fear, despite its negative hold, is really disguised energy centered amongst three powerful points of transformation.

> *All of my life I wanted to be somebody. Now, I see I should have been more specific.*
> **—Lily Tomlin**

Three Points of Transformation

Definitely, the wall of fear creates a block that surrounds the transformation of fear to energy, positive energy. To unmask critical aspects that surround your fear, reflect deeply on three points—

what you want, what you want to experience, and who you need to become. When you uncover the essence of the following three points, regardless of how impossible what you want may be at this time, the power to break down the wall of fear is ignited. In fact, you are revving your engine and getting ready to take off at the starting line.

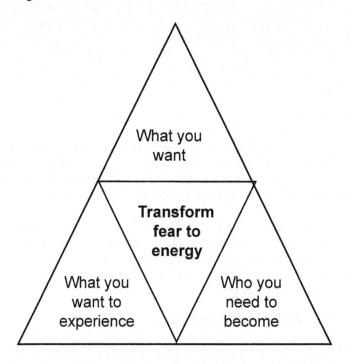

Energy Points of Transformation

1) What do you want?

Do you remember when you were a kid and you begged and pleaded and maybe even threw a tantrum when you really wanted something? My son had this technique down to an art. There was never any question of what he wanted, ever. The "I want" became part of his vocabulary at a very early age. What did you desire when you were five? How about at thirteen? Later, at twenty-one?

Maybe what you wanted changed slightly, but I would think you were able to describe what you wanted quite vividly. You also believed that you would get it. After all, isn't that what dreams are for?

How easily can you answer this question now? If your response is "I don't know," or "Just to be happy," then you are working too hard at remaining practical or you feel what you really want is not important because your family and friends have greater and more pressing needs and they are depending on you to take care of their needs. Someday, though, you can think about yourself but now, you can't.

Stop right there!

Deep down, you really know what you want. It may be hidden behind responsibilities, obligations, and daily survival, but it peeks out every once in a while. Give yourself permission to say what YOU want, not what others want for you but YOUR WANT.

If stating what you want is stressful, try this: whisper what you want, then say it a bit louder. Now, use your outside voice and declare what you want. One stipulation, though. You need to be specific. Envision what you want, feel what you want, and picture yourself having what you want.

2) What do you want to experience?

This question is a bit easier because this is a feeling you can intentionally seek out, and what you want to experience can occur in a variety of situations and settings. But the purpose of this question is not to consider a onetime occurrence; instead, what do you want to experience in your life, your work, and your relationships all of the time? The best way to answer this question is to think about what you are experiencing now compared to what you want to experience. How large is the gap? The gap, big or small, will give you a good view of how much work must be accomplished to close it.

3) Who do you need to become?

Your strengths, values, and character got you where you are today. You worked hard, achieved success, and developed a reputation. Suddenly, you realize what got you where you are now is not going to get you where you want to go. This is not a question of who you want to be. Who do you need to become means what strengths need to be developed, what new awareness of yourself must surface, and what challenges need to be conquered. This question is begging you to discover the real you, the person who will be answering the call to make great things happen.

Ready to Be Energized?

Remember, fear is energy that saps your drive, momentum, and spirit, and stops action. Yet at the same time, fear can be the energy necessary to give you a push out of your discomfort zone. What I mean is THAT your fear, when identified with what you are feeling, can be broken down by taking action, thereby lessening its negative control and increasing its positive control, similar to an adrenaline rush. It would seem the stronger you feel fear, the greater the transformation to energy, right? Well, yes and no. Let me tell you about Jessica.

Jessica was in much discomfort when she contacted me. I had known her for many years because we worked on several Chamber of Commerce committees together and we were both employed in banking at the time. Later, I lost touch with Jessica, until one day, I received an email from her. She'd learned from a newspaper article that I made a career transition and now helped people who were seeking meaning and purpose in their work. Jessica was glad to connect with me, sharing her discomfort of being in a job that was no longer rewarding, a draining work environment, and a general unhappiness. In fact, she had not been happy for a long time. After twenty-five years in her career, she wanted to change, not quite knowing where she hoped to go, but she knew she wanted something that gave her life deeper purpose.

Of course, Jessica had many walls of fear surrounding her ability to change. She had all of the motivation-sappers: fear of the unknown, of failure, of abandonment of the past, of what will people think—yes, all of them. Despite her fear, and with excitement, Jessica declared she was ready to change and wanted to transform her fears to energy.

So we began working to identify what she wanted, what she wanted to experience, and who she needed to become. Jessica struggled with the first question and would blame her lack of attention with the change process on her stress at work and busy family. Weeks would go by, and Jessica would continue this pattern of not being able to spend time in reflection or articulate what she wanted. All the time, she kept stating she truly desired to change careers and definitely wanted to do this.

Of course, the problem Jessica experienced was not a lack of desire to change. The unhappiness of where she was in her life was real and the thought of change made her hopeful, excited, and optimistic. But Jessica did not understand her intensity of discomfort in relation to her fears, and inadvertently set herself up for frustration, discouragement, and disappointment.

Recall that there are five fear generators creating walls:

1. The unknown

2. Failure

3. Abandonment

4. What others think

5. Success

In other words, how fear transforms to energy, breaking down walls and propelling you to action, is dependent upon understanding your discomfort level. Like Jessica, thinking about doing something different was exciting and she experienced no fear and little noticeable discomfort other than an itch. As we worked together and she was ready to take steps to actualize her dream, fears blocked her path; therefore, her discomfort increased. With fear in control, she chose inaction instead of action. Discomfort is gradual when you begin move from who you are to who you are meant to be. Knowing how you feel and understanding your readiness when experiencing discomfort will put you in control of your journey and help you move at a pace that is just right for you.

Breakthrough Exercise 4

Fear can be a wall that keeps you from achieving your goal or fear can be an adrenaline rush stirring your inner being and transforming life as you know it. Which one will you choose?

Here is an exercise to track how you are breaking down walls by transforming your fear to energy.

"A-ha/Oh-no" Journal

Catch yourself growing by keeping an A-ha/Oh-no journal.

Oh-no: Fears, limitations, and obstacles in your life as you embark on your journey of discovery.

A-ha: Challenges that you overcome, new perspectives, and hidden strengths that suddenly emerge.

Begin with a brand new, colorful notebook or if you prefer technology, create a spreadsheet. Make a list of the walls that are holding you back, the limitations making forward movement impossible. The wall, limitations, and fears are the "Oh-nos" of your life. So title your first page, "Oh-no," and start the list. Don't be surprised if the list is long: this means you are being totally honest about what is holding you back. The list will eventually shrink because you are converting every "Oh-no" to energy.

Next, title a page, "A-ha." At first, this page may be blank. If so moved, go ahead and add some color—doodle, decorate it. This page will hold power and energy and you want to give this page all of the fanfare you can. As you experience breakthroughs, change, and new behavior, record in the "A-ha" journal. With each breakthrough, refer to your "Oh-no" page, and identify which "Oh-no" is not an "Oh-no" anymore because you conquered the fear. Go ahead, draw a line right through or use a black magic marker to wipe the fear out. Oh, one more thing: make a note when your breakthrough appeared, and write down the date. What you will notice in a short time is the shorter intervals between breakthroughs. In turn, your skill for spotting opportunities to increase your "A-ha" moments becomes more proficient.

The exciting part of the "A-ha/Oh-no" journal is that you find the "A-ha" page fills up very fast and the "Oh-no" page dwindles away. Every time you add another "A-ha," you are transforming your fear to energy, and in turn, what you believed was a limitation was really an opportunity to breakdown the wall of fear and clearly see what is on the other side.

6 Old Thinking and New Thinking

If I knew where it was, I would take you there. But there is so much more than this.
—Eddie Vedder, "Breath"

Discomfort: the feeling you get when your shoes are too tight, or you are stuck in a cramped elevator going to the twentieth floor, or when you come in from a trenching rain because you forgot your umbrella at work. Ugh! That feeling is hard to ignore so kicking your shoes off, exiting the elevator, and changing to dry clothes immediately remedies the discomfort. For temporary, small discomfort the solution is simple. It's not as easy when it's hidden in a desire to change because that discomfort does not respond to obvious and known solutions. During times of change, without realizing what you are feeling is discomfort, your hopes and dreams for a new life can alter from excitement to fear to confusion. By the time you reach utter chaos, you have abandoned all desire to change. Emotionally and mentally exhausted and drained by fear, you remain where you are, nice and safe.

Stuck in Old Thinking

Surprisingly, getting what you want, having the experience you want, and becoming who you are meant to be, is possible and achievable. Really. The problem that most people who want to follow their calling to greater purpose experience is being stuck in outdated thinking. They believe that in order to make change happen, even a much desired change, leaving their comfort zone is the only option. That type of thinking will get you nowhere fast. Just the thought of leaving a place of comfort to enter a place unknown, unstable, and uncomfortable, is, well, stupid and irresponsible. Yet, with old thinking, you know the time will come to leave your comfort zone. You prepare for a sensible decision and gauge your timing. Then again, not in the immediate future because you need more time to train, to become an expert, and to build a new network of friends and colleagues. Your list becomes longer and longer and longer. All the while, you keep waiting for your confidence level to increase. And waiting, and waiting.

I am going to reiterate a really important statement here, so listen closely. Read it aloud. Let your voice commit it to memory.

Your comfort zone is an illusion. There is no comfort zone and you are not residing in comfort because there is none when you have the itch to change. Instead, where you are existing is a discomfort zone and remaining in a state of discomfort is uncomfortable.

This is old thinking: *Change can only happen if I leave my comfort zone.*

This is new thinking: *Change can only happen if I leave my discomfort zone.*

Can you see the difference? Certainly, if you are experiencing discomfort (and you are), you want to stop the discomfort, ease the pain, and feel good again. In old thinking, what you believe to be your comfort zone—that is, what is familiar, not challenging, known stuff—is not comfort, but really *habits*. When you consider even a slight thought about doing something different, you have unknowingly triggered the first stage of discomfort.

In reality, there are five stages of discomfort you will experience as you move from who you are to who you are meant to be. Each stage has distinct characteristics and knowing what stage of discomfort you are experiencing is critical in designing a strategy with actions steps to achieve short- and long-term goals. If you search Amazon.com, you will find literally thousands of self-help books offering change techniques, comprehensive plans with ten steps, twelve steps, two steps, or any other combination of anecdotal- or evidence-based approaches. Every approach guarantees help with making the changes you desire in your life. Many of the approaches are useful, some are costly, and others free. I have a bookshelf filled with every conceivable technique for changing my life, finding true happiness, achieving success, acquiring unbelievable wealth, and becoming the best that I can be. The problem with most techniques is the assumption that if you are reading the book, you want to change. Well, you probably do . . . well, sort of. *Maybe.* Okay, you want to change but somehow following the plan does not equip you with a good dose of hope, or the steps may be a struggle to master. So what do you next? Buy another book, try something new, or give up because you seriously think what you really need is professional therapy.

What is occurring while you are following a change plan, regardless of how great the plan or how many amazing testimonials boast of success and turning points, is that your level of discomfort determines your behavior and your fear factor. Regardless of your desire to change, nothing will make a difference if you do not understand what discomfort stage you are experiencing and apply techniques appropriate for what stage you are in. The five stages of discomfort can be described in two ways: what your inner voice is telling you and how you behave.

Five Stages of Discomfort

Stage 1: Exploration

Inner voice words: *I need something different in my life.*

This is the first stage of discomfort and certainly one of the most enjoyable stages, because the possibilities are endless; you can visualize an exciting, new lifestyle, career, and relationships. Your imagination goes wild because, well, you can. Nobody really knows you are in this stage. It is your secret. This stage is non-threatening, and exhibits the following characteristics:

- Fun
- Discovery
- Exciting
- Safe
- Comfortable
- Daydreaming
- Envisioning a new self

Stage 2: Tinkering

Inner voice words: *Go ahead try one new thing. Just wiggle your toes to test the water.*

In this stage, you want to see movement, but not too much because, after all, you are not ready to change yet. Of course, if a job offer fell in your lap complete with a six-figure salary, unbelievable perks, a company car, and unlimited travel expense (keep watching the sky), you would change in a heartbeat. Nice, now snap out of it. This stage disturbs your status quo just enough to have you buckle your seatbelt as your emotions begin a roller coaster climb. The characteristics of this stage are:

- Hopeful but anxious

- Excited but uncertain

- Think about change often

- Talk about change to close family and select group of friends

- Monitor your behavior so not to raise any suspicions of change

Stage 3: Chaotic Confusion

Inner voice words: Go back: who are you? You don't belong any-where—why did you think you could change?

This is the most critical stage because of the feeling of loss of control. How could this be happening, because you always knew what you were doing and where you were headed? Now uncertainty and confusion are ever-present, who you were is not working, and the new you seems awkward and uncomfortable. This stage is the best environment for your inner voice to thrive by reminding you that you are not good enough, you are an imposter, and who do you think you are, anyway? Of course, holding conversations with your inner voice allows your confidence level to dip lower and lower as time passes in this stage. Because the discomfort in this stage is so intense, you may lose sight of your goal because who you are is not aligned with what you are doing. Emotional waves, up and down, has you descending on a steep slope, and you are trying to hang on tight. By now, your only thought is, "How do I stop this madness?" You want to go back, yet you want to move forward; all the while, movement seems to be in slow motion, and your unpredictable behavior has a direct impact on your friends and family. They want the old you back, the "you" they knew, whoever that was, you are not even sure. The intensity in this stage is great and can launch you into any one of the five fears easily. You must give yourself permission to just "hang out" here for a short time. The characteristics of this stage are:

- Cannot go forward
- Cannot go backward
- No longer belong to the past
- The present is unclear
- The future is unknown

Your inner voice is having a great time making you feel inadequate, not confident, inept, lost, and just plain lousy.

Stage 4: Breathing

Inner voice words joined with your thoughts: *I know who I am—everything is beginning to make sense and I know where I am headed.*

In this stage, breakthroughs are evident in your thinking and your actions. The path to achieving your goal is much smoother than in any other stage and your values, your passion, and who you are meant to be are emerging in your work and in your life. You believe your calling is beginning to crystalize, and a sense of calm, not chaos, is directing your behavior. Without much effort, new opportunities appear, and somehow, you know something great is about to happen. Time to not only breathe, but to exhale and sigh. The characteristics of this stage are:

- Smiling
- Laughing
- Confidence
- Sense of accomplishment
- Doors are opening that never opened before

Stage 5: Victorious

What you are thinking (no inner voice): *I am ready to take on greater challenges.*

This is the stage you have been awaiting a long time. Reaching this makes all of the other stages worth the discomfort, because you now know what a real comfort zone feels like. Not a habit, not living on autopilot, not moving mechanically through the day, but real comfort in knowing you are, while following your calling, and your strengths, passion, values, and purpose, working in unison with your life's work. Take a moment to feel the warmth of being victorious and enjoy every moment knowing you are stronger, wiser, and more confident than ever and getting better and better every day. The characteristics of this stage are:

- Passionate
- Value-driven
- Creative
- Sense of gratitude
- Happy

The Stage of Your Life

Countless research studies have been conducted on change because the topic demands to be studied. Change and the way people and organizations approach, experience, react, and accept what is happening is fascinating and many studies have led to change theories. Certainly, one of the most popular change theories was developed by James O. Prochaska, PhD. In his book, *Changing for Good: A Revolutionary Six-Stage Program for Overcoming Bad Habits and Moving Your Life Positively Forward* (Avon Books, 1995), Prochaska provides a six-step program designed for people who want to change bad habits, such as addictions, eating, smoking, or any behavior detrimental to a positive, healthy lifestyle.

Though his research was directed at discovering how people used tools to make changes in their life, his breakthrough discovery of the stages of change occurred because of *when* people used the tools, not *how*. Prochaska considered various behaviors in the change process and movement identified as stages that eventually led to successful goal achievement. Beginning with a pre-contemplation stage and progressing to a termination stage, people would not necessarily move effortlessly through each stage. Instead, people who wanted to change were stuck in one for a long time, moved backwards instead of forward, or experienced staggered movement. Some people stopped and started over many times with little progress or even a sudden surge in progress. Again, achieving a goal of changing a bad habit was not the result of the tool being used. Goal achievement was dependent on the stage of readiness for the participant to use tools effectively.

In a similar manner, when you decide that something is missing from your work and life, and you want to follow your calling to discover meaning and purpose, you experience stages of discomfort. Ideally, you begin with a slight itch, a possibility—after all, you are just exploring. Next, you take some small, nonthreatening actions. Here you are Tinkering, still not in much discomfort. That is, until you move into unfamiliar territory, and find your life to be in upheaval. Discomfort is painful, and need I say it: you are in Chaotic Confusion. Of course, as change takes hold, and opportunities appear, your discomfort lessens, and you can breathe again. Wait, one more: you are Victorious when your vision finally becomes reality.

However, progression through the various stages of discomfort might not be linear. If fact, movement may even cease, giving you the feeling of being stuck, or movement may bounce back and forth, leading to confusion, frustration, and discouragement. Most important is to know what level of discomfort you are experiencing and to allow time in each stage of discomfort to determine the walls of fear blocking your progress. Only then can you choose the right tools of support to guide your progression to the last stage, Victorious. Gaining an understanding of the stages of discomfort in relation to what you are feeling and what is directing your emotion, your logic, and your behavior puts you in control of designing change at your own pace, your own timeline, and your own comfort.

Where Are You?

After reviewing the five stages of discomfort, can you simply pinpoint what stage you are experiencing? Lucky you if you selected stage five, and you are Victorious and enjoying all the wonders of being you. I would suppose, more than likely, you are closer to stage one, two, or the dreaded stage three. Be assured that you will get to stage four and eventually stage five, and when you do, you will look back at your journey and know that every stage was a learning experience, and you have gained inner wisdom and awareness of how unique and special you really are.

In the meantime, what is important is that you understand your level of discomfort as described in the stages because this awareness will give you control and help you navigate the path to discovering greater meaning and purpose in your work and life. One of the easiest ways to identify what stage you are in is to listen to your inner voice, because that voice has a variety of stage personalities making an appearance when the time is right.

As a child, I never had an imaginary friend or an imaginary pet; the thought of talking to air or a phantom person or animal never crossed my mind. Of course, since I attended parochial school, the nuns would always make me and the other students leave a little room on our seats for our guardian angel. Thank goodness my guardian angel was skinny because I never left her too much room, and if I forgot she was with me, I had visions of her being squashed. What an awful thought! I would have to go through life without a guardian angel.

However, when my inner voice made its debut in the Exploration stage when I was contemplating a career change, we became very good friends. Finally, I found the imaginary friend that I never had as a child. Because we became such good friends, I named her Matilda. She was motivating and encouraging, and whispered, "This is exciting, go ahead, see the vision," and, "You deserve to get what you want, you are great, go for it." When I moved to the Tinkering stage, Matilda was present but altered her personality, being more logical and cautious: making me feel slightly anxious, telling me to just try sending out my resume or try to meet new people, but don't go too far because you are not ready. Guess what? By the time I reached the Chaotic Confusion stage, Matilda's personality changed drastically and instead of being my best imaginary friend, her demeanor was cruel, rude, disgusting, and hurtful. I listened to every word and believed Matilda spoke the truth. I think she really enjoyed seeing me in such confusion and chaos because she could tell me anything and I believed her. Thank goodness that by the time I reached the Breathing stage, Matilda's personality became more pleasant, and in fact, I think she took a vacation at that time because I didn't hear much from her. In the Victorious stage, Matilda and I have reached an understanding about how and when we can have a conversation and we both agreed she is at her best when her personality is motivating, energizing, and positive.

In order to know what stage you are experiencing, use the personality of your inner voice as a measurement. Listen closely to what your inner voice is telling you over and over again. What conversation are you having with your inner voice and how do you feel after the conversation? Is your imaginary friend, your inner voice, being your best friend ever, or is it being a bully and calling you names? Measure your inner voice and you will know your stage.

Where Do You Want to Be?

If level of discomfort determines movement, waiting to feel the pain may be deceiving because in the Exploration stage, you feel good, but you do not want to be stuck in daydreaming. When you are Tinkering, the discomfort is mild, but again, you do not want to just dabble, you want movement. Of course, by the time you get to the Chaotic Confusion and you want to move, your discomfort is downright annoying, and as hard as you try, movement is difficult, to say the least. If you long to be in the Breathing and Victorious stage, the stage where discomfort transforms to comfort, you must first understand where you are, where you want to be, and what challenges you will face. Moving from stage to stage is possible, and the best part is that you determine how and when you move, so the Victorious stage is within reach, regardless of which one you're in right now.

Breakthrough Exercise 5

Discomfort does not necessarily mean pain or causing pain. In fact, discomfort, particularly in the first stage (Exploration), can be quite exciting. Knowing what stage of discomfort you are experiencing gives you a place to begin movement, a place to draw a mark in the sand and to leave an impression of your footprints of where you have been as you move toward your goal.

Pinpoint Your Place

Review each of the characteristics of the five stages of discomfort:

- Exploration
- Tinkering
- Chaotic Confusion
- Breathing
- Victory

At various times, you may find you experience characteristics of two stages. This is where your inner voice can be helpful. Think about your conversations with your inner voice, and determine if you feel more energized or more drained after spending quality time discussing you. Now, imagine the stages of discomfort as if they were displayed on a wall map, and place your pin on the discomfort stage location of where you are at right now.

There: you have a beginning point and are ready to move forward.

Of course, you want your movements to be directed toward reaching the Victorious stage so you need to create a future self.

Metaphorically Speaking

A metaphor creates a powerful vision of what you are feeling and allows you to communicate your feelings through recognizable objects, situations, or actions. A metaphor gives your feelings validity, and provides comfort because the feeling is familiar, even if the feeling is not pleasant.

Think about where you are at in the discomfort stage (Stage 1, 2, 3, 4, or 5), and associate what you are feeling with a familiar and similar feeling that you had experienced in the past.

Finish this phrase: *As I move from who I am to who I am meant to be, I feel like* _____

_____

_____

_____

Hint: You can even a draw a picture if you like!

Speak metaphorically every month; that is, do this exercise every thirty days, and pay close attention to how your metaphor changes. The difference in what you are feeling and how you describe the feeling will help you become very aware of how your thinking is changing. Suggestion: You can do this exercise each time you eliminate an "Oh-no" transaction with an "A-ha" moment to visually feel the change occurring.

7 Moving from Stage to Stage

Destiny is not a matter of chance, but of choice. Not something to wish for, but to attain.
—William Jennings Bryan

By now, you probably have a pretty good idea of what discomfort stage you are experiencing and you are anxious to get moving or else you would have dismissed any thoughts of change long ago. Or you might have chalked up what you were feeling to the normal aging process, an attack of the midlife crisis, knowing it will pass, and you can go back to your normal routine. But surprisingly, what you are feeling did not disappear. Your feelings are real, and try as you may, your inner voice will not let you ignore the discomfort. So is it time to get moving?

When Are You Ready?

Here is a simple test: listen closely—whose voice do you hear? Is that your inner voice whispering words of encouragement? Maybe the pesky inner voice is shouting words of defeat, and you want to agree? Maybe what you hear are your friends giving you advice on making a change or rationalizing why change is not good for you.

How about your family? What are you hearing from them? After all, your family has your best interest at heart, so you should listen. Really, are you sure? Or is their discomfort adding to yours?

If you are listening to a voice other than your own, and you are thinking that you should move, you are not ready to move.

> *The keyword here is SHOULD. Never should on yourself.*
> —**Vicki Austin**, career coach and professional speaker

When you decide you *should* move to another stage, what you are doing is listening to someone else, not you. Who knows what is best for you? You value advice and feedback, but the decision, the timing, and your readiness is up to you, not anyone else. When you are ready, you will know.

For the longest time, I believed my son would enter kindergarten still wearing diapers. I tried every game, every trick I knew to get him to use the potty. My daughter was so easy, I figured using the same techniques would work like a charm. Dancing, running water, toys in the bathroom, snacks, even reading a story about Potty Pete, but nothing worked. He was not going to use the potty, and that was that. I told him many times, "You *should* be using the potty, like a big boy." Guess how that approach worked?

Then one morning, I walked into his room; he had just awoken. To my surprise, his diaper was dry. Okay, could this be the day? I lifted him from the crib and we walked (I was running and he followed) to the bathroom. I could not get the diaper off fast enough. I then set him on his potty, and success. What a wonderful sound: *tinkle, tinkle, tinkle.* Time for a happy dance, a big hug, a gold star, and fireworks. In his own time, he was ready to move to the next stage: wearing Batman underwear.

Movement Habits

Of course, having a desire to move through the stages is the start but actually creating movement is much more difficult. You want to move beyond the Exploration stage, and really want to get out the Chaotic Confusion stage, but you are stuck, there are so many obstacles, and at this point, you are overwhelmed.

For this reason, developing habits that keep you moving forward would be well worth your time and effort. New behavior repeated over and over helps you maintain control even when everything around you is changing. The purpose of creating habits, positive habits, instead of following steps is that habits become your natural behavior, deep-seated in your lifestyle, and will impact all facets of your life. Steps, on the other hand, are usually applied in a process, and once the process is complete, the steps are no longer useful. For this reason, here are five important habits you want to begin developing now.

Habit 1: Create Urgency

Time moves quickly and before you realize what happened, a day, a week, a month, a year is gone. Whether you decide to move through the stages of change or just sit idly daydreaming, time will pass, and you can look back and be glad you decided to move, or you can shake your head in regret for being complacent and doing nothing. The habit of urgency prioritizes the speed of movement and gives your movement purpose.

After all, John Kotter, an expert on change in organizations, believes that urgency is the driving force to get people to move in the direction of change instead of moving away from change and creating unnecessary resistance. Kotter, in his book, *The Heart of Change: Real-Life Stories of How People Change Their Organizations* (Harvard Business Review Press, 2012), explains that without a sense of urgency, priority, and purpose, there is no reason to change today, tomorrow, or ever. By creating a story, an eye-opening problem that exists, and highlighting the benefits of a solution, change in an organization becomes necessary, and taking action now instead of later is important to everyone, not just one person.

Likewise, you want to develop a habit of urgency in moving from stage, but not urgent in the sense that you move even when you are not ready. You create urgency with identifying a problem and solution that will put you in better place if you apply the solution.

Let me explain. When I was working on my doctorate, I set a goal of completing all of my coursework, including my comprehensive exam and dissertation, in three years. The program was designed to be completed in four years, which meant I needed to double up my coursework if I was to accomplish a doctorate in three years. The urgency was not that I was getting older (I tried not to keep reminding myself), but that I wanted my mother to see me graduate as a doctor. At the end of the three years it would take me to complete the program, my mother would be eighty-eight years old. I kept thinking, what if she is not around to see me walk down the aisle on graduation day and hear the university president call me "Doctor"? The obvious concern was she was not going to get younger, and I wanted her to hear the band play "Pomp and Circumstance" as I walked the graduation red carpet, one more time, the last time. My urgency, making my mother proud of me after I put her through hell as a teenager, was the driving force that pushed me through stages of discomfort. I am happy I created urgency because my mother was in the audience as I delivered the student graduation commencement speech and was announced as Dr. Susan Neustrom.

Habit 2: Choose Your Move

Whether you realize it or not, you are not the same person you were before deciding change was necessary. Your thoughts, actions, and behavior are different, even if others cannot detect the change. You can. Believe it or not, because your thoughts are now different, you have the option to choose when you want to move from stage to stage. Really. The habit of choosing your move, not when you *should or should not* (someone telling you what to do), but when the time is right. This is your personal choice. Isn't that a great habit to develop?

Too bad Sherri did not develop the habit, because she had such big ambitions and dreams that probably will never materialize. Sherri built a career in manufacturing, and after twelve years working for one company, she was laid off. Sherri was devastated, but at the same time realized she finally had an opportunity to pursue her dream: Sherri wanted to be a teacher. She understood that returning to school to earn a teaching degree and certificate would be first, but she really did not mind, even though she admitted school at age forty-five would be awkward. But her dream of being a teacher would actually come true.

With this in mind, Sherri began exploring opportunities where she might begin her new career and universities offering teaching programs. Sherri spoke frequently about how her vision of teaching began at an early age. Life has a way of changing plans, however: she never had the opportunity to pursue college because she got married, had kids, and with bills, mortgage, and family, her dreams were just that, a dream to be put on hold indefinitely. Of course, while in the Exploration stage, Sherri continued to apply for jobs in manufacturing because she knew the industry, she knew her job, everything was familiar, with no challenges. Change was exciting as Sherri dreamed of finally teaching and I worked with her to take action steps to move to the Tinkering stage. Whenever Sherri had the urge to move, she would tell me she couldn't because her husband wanted her to get a job first, or her mother didn't think she should change careers, or her friends would suggest other more lucrative careers than teaching. For Sherri, choosing to move was not a personal choice but a *should* choice and she chose not move from the Exploration stage because she should take care of everyone's needs, not her needs. When Sherri received an offer from another manufacturing company, doing the same job she did in her past company, Sherri accepted. Sherri remains employed in manufacturing, and following her calling of teaching is still in the Exploration stage, ten years later.

Habit 3: Move By Inches, Not Feet

When you look out to the horizon from the vantage point of where you are now, peeking at where you want to be, how long is the distance? Even if you squint, point A to point B is pretty darn far away. That view can be in such a very distant future that you want to abandon your journey even before you start. Developing the habit of moving by inches, not feet, will enable you to move on a steady pace, all the while making progress and taking in the beautiful scenery as you inch your way through your life-changing journey.

Nothing supports the concept of inches, not feet, like the kaizen (Japanese word meaning "good change") philosophy. Robert Maurer, PhD, author of *The Spirit of Kaizen: Creating Lasting Excellence One Small Step at a Time* (McGraw-Hill, 2012), shares specific stories of organizations that applied a kaizen strategy, the power of small steps, in creating change. Again and again, the result was major breakthroughs in employee behavior and thinking allowing change to occur.

Similarly, Jim Collins, in his classic book, *Good to Great: Why Some Companies Make the Leap . . . And Others Don't* (Harper Business, 2001), describes how companies that were doing well appeared to accelerate to greatness. The change from good to great did not suddenly happen. There was not one particular, dramatic action that turned the company around. Rather, small steps created consistent, steady movement, the kaizen strategy: inches, not feet.

The reason kaizen works is because it is comfortable and doable. Dr. Maurer is quick to point out that change is frightening and our bodies are hard-wired to take flight when danger is present. Your body's immediate reaction to change is to shut down and do nothing, to hide, to run. Fear takes over, and you know how limiting fear can be. Taking small steps does not produce the same reaction because movement is slow, paced, comfortable, and continuous. Strike a balance between movement and a sense of urgency with consistency of progress.

By using the kaizen philosophy to maintain motion, moving to the next stage becomes effortless and more enjoyable. In fact, movement is subtle, and your creativity is in high gear so much, you cannot even notice a turning point from one stage to the next. Moving by inches, not feet, soothes your discomfort, and allows you to enjoy your discovery journey.

Habit 4: Amplify Your Self-Awareness

One of the most fascinating studies you will ever encounter is the study of YOU, opening your eyes to why you do the things you do, why people interact with you as they do, and how you are perceived by others is a never ending quest for self-discovery. For me, one of the highlights of working with students is to introduce them to reflective exercises and observe a sudden shift in thinking, allowing new perspectives about their behavior to surface. Exercises that open a window into your feelings, thoughts, and actions are powerful change methods that reap incredible results and lead to greater self-efficacy and self-confidence. So, I guess convincing you to create a habit to increase your self-awareness is a no-brainer. Maybe. Learn to recognize queues and triggers. Look at yourself objectively. Multiple assessments are available to test your personality, and every one of them has value and offers a certain degree of value and insight to who you are.

However, becoming self-aware goes beyond taking a standardized assessment and reading the results of your responses to a hundred-question (or more) survey. Deep self-awareness is a continuous workout of clarifying your values, challenging the origin of your long-held beliefs, and taking responsibility for your actions. Through reflection, journaling, and honest feedback, you will learn more about yourself than you ever thought possible, and you will see a new you, the hidden you. In spite of how well you think you know yourself now, amplifying your self-awareness is one of the best habits to develop, especially as you move from the stage that creates the most discomfort, stage three, chaotic confusion.

Certainly, one of the most significant twenty-first century leadership books is *True North: Discover Your Authentic Leadership* (Jossey-Bass, 2007). Author Bill George, former CEO of Metronic for ten years, interviewed 125 great leaders to gain an understanding of leadership styles and success. Surprisingly, George discovered few similarities in leadership character, skills, and talents. Instead, great leaders described the one "a-ha" moment, a turning point when they became totally self-aware of their authentic self and were able to lead with purpose and passion. George equates deep self-awareness to the layers of an onion: as you peel away the layers of who you are, under each layer, you discover a different aspect of you. When you finally get close to your center, you are experiencing the real you that has not yet surfaced in the world. He describes this core as your authentic self. As seemingly easy as the description sounds, finding your authentic self creates much anxiety. Your first reaction, of course, is fear, and you want to shield your center with a false you, a fabricated version of who you really are. Thus, you experience Chaotic Confusion, because you have peeled away multiple layers of you (the onion) that have been growing very well over the years.

So in essence, a battle is taking place between the layers: your attitude, behavior, and persona that has served you, so far, and your core, the authentic you. Which one is stronger? If you create a habit of amplifying your self-awareness, I think you can predict the winner. Once the core, the real you, emerges in victory, you will need to take some time to get acquainted with this person, because the more sociable you get, the faster you will propel toward your vision.

Habit 5: Use Your Vision as a Guide

See your vision, feel your vision, and know your vision. Even if it seems light-years away and next to impossible, your vision holds your purpose, passion, and potential. Furthermore, your vision is there for a reason, and although right now you may have doubts about the likelihood of your vision becoming reality, make a habit of using your vision as a guide for selecting opportunities, building relationships, and to actually say no to everyone's request of your time. If you try to use logic, money, prestige, or anything besides your vision and your energy, motivation and persistence will be difficult to maintain as you move through the stages of discomfort.

To put it another way, I tossed my GPS long ago because I kept arguing with the know-it-all woman inside the device. Can you believe it? She wanted me to make a legal U-turn on the expressway! Instead of watching the exit, I was arguing with the voice on my dashboard. The last straw was searching for a community college around sixty miles from my house because I had arranged for an informational interview and hoped to make a good connection. Following the voice, the endpoint was a farmhouse in the middle of nowhere: just corn, cows, and lots of hay, *not* the college. Try searching for a gas station or police in the middle of a cornfield. I drove far out of my way to find directions from a local store clerk. Not only was I late for my appointment, but I was so frustrated, discouraged, and stressed, that anything shared in the interview was not really important because I was so mad at myself for not using more dependable directions.

By the same token, not using your vision as a guide can lead you in a direction you do not want to go and you might end up in a place far removed from your original destination. To make a habit of using your vision as a guide, always ask yourself three questions before deciding to take action.

1. Will this action move me an inch closer to my vision?

2. Am I choosing this action or do I "should" this action?

3. What will I learn about myself with this action?

Moving through the stages of discomfort is more focused when your vision is clear, your path is not cluttered with limitations, and you have a strategy with a plan of action.

Go ahead, post a statement of your vision on your wall, on your computer, your bathroom mirror, or anywhere where it will be noticeable all the time. Now you can begin to move knowing you have a lighthouse to guide you on your journey. Take heart, because when you develop the habit of using your vision as a guide, you will arrive at your destination with less frustration and stress than by using any other guide.

Habits are formed through repetition, and when practiced regularly, become as routine as brushing your teeth. In a very short time, the discomfort you feel will no longer be a lingering pain. Instead, habits provide soothing relief, like a warm blanket, a hot cup of chamomile tea, or wind chimes on a warm, breezy summer day. In a state of calmness, self-confidence, and lessened stress, you can move from stage to stage, all the while becoming who you are meant to be.

Breakthrough Exercise 6

Habit-Forming Habits

1. Create urgency

   a. List all of the reasons why reaching the Victorious stage is important

   b. Now with each reason, ask yourself, "Why?" and continue this process until you get to the core of the urgency. The core, the real urgency, is hidden inside a reason, and when you find it, you will move steadily.

2. Choose your move

   a. When you decide to take action, stop and describe the action and why you are taking it.

   b, Did you say you *should* in your description? If you hear the word "should," even if it's coming from you inner voice, rethink your action and only move when <u>you want</u> to move, not because you *should* move.

3. Move by inches

   a. What can you accomplish in fifteen minutes that would move you closer to your goal? Do an inch task every day, the Kaizen strategy.

   b. Keep a calendar handy (paper or electronic) to track your daily inch task. In an average month, doing a fifteen-minute inch task equates to 450 minutes, or 7.5 hours.

4. Self-awareness

   a. Complete the following phrases

      i. I am at my best when . . .

      ii. I feel active and alive when . . .

      iii. I have a deep sense of purpose when . . .

   b. Now read each phrase. How often are you engaged in activities that bring out the best of you, when you're active and alive and have a deep sense of purpose?

c. Get a large poster board and catch yourself doing each of the phrases. Then write down the activity and date on a sticky note and stick to the poster. One word of advice: as you move closer to the Victorious stage, you will may need to buy about five more large posters.

5. Vision

a. Imagining your vision is good. Stating your vision is better. Creating your vision is best. Here is an interesting way to design your future self. Write a resume in the future, as if each accomplishment and achievement occurred just as you imagined it would.

Future-Self Resume: Creating the Vision

When you begin your journey of discovery, whatever stage you begin from, the goal may seem so far away and out of reach. A life filled with purpose, passion, and potential is achievable, yet not easy to embrace. Creating a "future-self resume" is a motivating exercise and helps you identify your strengths, values, and exciting possibilities, and creates a compelling vision. The great thing about a future-self resume is you can include as many accomplishments as you want, because, well, they're your accomplishments in the future. Go ahead, write that future resume with all the bells and whistles, professional summary, accomplishments, experience, education, awards, and anything else that would motivate and inspire you to keep moving. Write them as you want them to be, not as you think they *should* be.

When you have completed the future-self resume, keep it close at hand because you will need to view the resume during your journey of discovery to continually keep you motivated to pursue your goal.

The Comfort Zone Illusion

Chapter

8 Something Great Is About to Happen

One does not discover new lands without consenting to lose sight of the shore for a very long time.
—André Gide

Reinvent yourself! Everyone uses this phrase for describing transformation. I always want to ask, reinvent what? And why do I need to reinvent me? If I reinvent myself, what happens to the emerging real me, the "me" that is battling with my old self? Do I reinvent and become a different person? Do I reinvent to act and think like other people believe I *should*? Remember the problem with *should*? I see an issue with the entire reinvent concept.

As a matter of fact, a "reinvent yourself" search on Amazon.com yielded approximately 2,465 titles referencing reinvention of some sort. There is even an *Idiot's Guide* to the subject. I suppose even idiots want to change something, although I can only imagine their true ambitions. Okay, one more check of Amazon, and, yes, there is a reinvent book for dummies. Now I know I really dislike the label, "reinvent." My personal belief is that "reinvent" is a clever, much promising marketing word that sells books, programs, and tools. And of course, even an idiot or a dummy can benefit from reinvention. From a standpoint of change, reinvent describes people who are tired of who they are and want to do something new. To reinvent yourself also implies you can change like a chameleon to fit into a new situation, job, or life. Later, when you are tired of your color, reinvent yourself again and again. There are certainly enough how-to, steps, programs, and advice out there to do this over 2,000 times. To me, reinvent sounds like a lot of work and what if it doesn't work very well? Do I need to demolish my invention and start over? Ugh! Is reinvention what you want?

Or are you truly seeking a life with purpose, meaning, and passion doing work that matters and creating a legacy? If so, you are not seeking to reinvent yourself, improve yourself, become a new you, or create a different brand. The discomfort you are feeling did not originate from boredom, or from seeking adventure, or even from what some may call your "midlife crisis." Your discomfort stems from your core, the authentic you, the one that has been hidden for a long time between the layers of the many roles you play in your life. So reinventing yourself will only mask your discomfort and soon your authentic self will be banging on your mind again wanting to get out.

Think about it. Now, at this particular time, the authentic you, is ready to emerge if you give it a chance. Why is this true? Because otherwise, you would not be feeling discomfort, not have daily or sometimes hourly conversations with your inner voice, or not be envisioning a change. In other words, hold on, something great is getting ready to happen, and you don't want to muddle it with a reinvention.

Journey of Discovery

Your next question is probably, "How?" I am glad you are ready to get moving, so try not think in terms of a process, program, or steps you monitor because your first thought would be to follow a set of rules, procedures, and strategies in a defined order for change to occur. Constructing your life for great things to happen is not process, a track, or a procedure, but rather, an exciting journey.

Can you recall a journey, a vacation, or a short trip you will never forget and every time you view photos and share your memories, you are happy, excited, alive, energized, and feeling inner peace and contentment? Maybe it was a recent trip or possibly a childhood vacation where you often revisit in your mind. Take a moment now and visualize the experience. Stay there for a while, breathe, and relax. Where did your mind take you? How do you feel?

That same memorable journey is what you are about to embark upon. Imagine where you are at right now, at whatever stage of discomfort you find yourself, as the beginning of a journey. On your journey, you will be visiting places you do not know well, so you stop and investigate, and time will pass, but you are not stalled, wasting your time, or depleting your energy. What you are doing is taking in the moment (even if the moment is frustrating); therefore, movement in the sense of moving forward may not appear to be happening. In reality, movement is actually occurring on a deep level, behind the scenes, so to speak, and the subtleness of the changes you are experiencing is what makes the journey so exciting.

The first thing to remember is that each destination along the journey is significant and will coincide with your discomfort stage. That is, your readiness to move from one discomfort stage to the next will get a good push when you are engaged in a journey of discovery instead of a process of change. As with any journey, you want to take in the scenery, relax, enjoy the experience, and eventually reach your destination. So with that intent in mind, following a process or procedure is not what you want to do because you will miss so many of the beautiful places along the way. I guarantee the journey of discovery will be a turning point in your life and take you to places that you could only dream about. But now these places and experiences are real.

Connecting the Destinations

By now, you have pinpointed the stage of discomfort in which you are residing. You understand your walls of fear. You are developing the five habits necessary for taking action. Everything you have done so far is in preparation for intentional movement, the type of movement that results in action, accomplishment, and finally, victory. Anything worth doing involves hard work. Designing your life for great things to happen requires commitment, focus, and dedication to the journey of reaching not only your short-term goals, but also achieving your long-term goals and beyond. Actually, what you are doing is creating a lifetime of habits and actions that continue to move you closer and closer to your ideal life. The trick, of course, is to enjoy the journey, instead of painfully following a plan of change that feels uncomfortable, awkward, and just not *you*. Of course, both methods will more than likely help you reach a goal. One method is life-changing, while the latter method is "in the moment change." If the experience is painful, the likelihood of creating long-lasting change is doubtful. Let's say you were given a choice—which method is more appealing?

To begin your journey of discovery, you will need to have an itinerary to follow so you can spend some time understanding where you will be going, what you will be doing, and how long you want to visit a destination. You will be making six stops along the way as you create your ideal life. With each stop, you will be taking photos, and collecting souvenirs, gold nuggets, and fresh perspectives, and generating unbelievable energy and excitement. You may even decide to revisit some of the stops several times before you travel to your next destination. This is perfectly fine, since you are in control of your journey, and the scope of your discovery may be deeply hidden in a particular destination. You will need to find the treasure before moving on.

Are you ready for your journey of discovery? You may be feeling a bit anxious and that's fine. Don't worry because the journey begins rather comfortably, allowing you to ease into a good pace and frame of mind, and you will quickly see a variety of new places to explore.

Journey of Discovery Itinerary

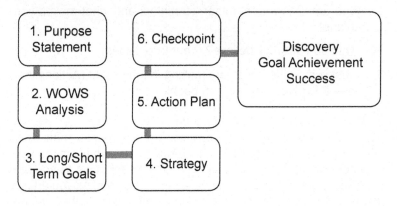

1. Purpose Statement
2. WOWS Analysis
3. Long/Short Term Goals
4. Strategy
5. Action Plan
6. Checkpoint
Discovery Goal Achievement Success

Roads of Destination

Destination 1: Write your purpose statement

Travel to this destination when you are in discomfort zone one, Exploration.

A purpose statement is not about your job or your position in a company. Instead, a purpose statement is about you, your work (not employment), and what gives your life meaning. You are a person of character, value, and strengths, regardless of your role. The outcome of developing a purpose statement is worth the time and effort because you understand yourself on a deeper level, truly know your strengths, and tap into the core of what excites and energizes you.

Your purpose statement should answer three questions.

1. Who am I? (Your character, strengths, and what makes you unique)

2. What do I strongly believe? (Your true values)

3. What is the difference I am making in the world? (Actions that have a significant impact on people)

Creating a purpose statement need not be a tedious exercise. Sit in silence and let your mind envision your purpose. Then write what you feel, what you know to be true, and what makes you truly come alive. No need to write complete sentences as you are thinking; jot down words, phrases, even metaphors. As you articulate your purpose, the words will come and meld together to form a perfect purpose statement. When you are satisfied with defining your purpose, create a card, flyer, or poster of it and place it where you will be able to view it every day. Use your imagination and be creative with designing a place for your purpose statement. As your first destination, the purpose statement is your guide for all destinations on your journey of discovery.

Destination 2: WOWS Analysis

Travel this destination when you are in discomfort zone one, Exploration, or zone two, Tinkering.

Next, you will analyze yourself from a future perspective, and create a framework for designing your goals that can be accomplished rather quickly and goals that are not ready to materialize yet. Unlike a conventional SWOT (Strengths, Weaknesses, Opportunities, and Threats) analysis used by many organizations in strategic planning, the WOWS analysis is not concerned with your current strengths, weakness, or threats. Instead, WOWS is evaluating your wants, opportunities, outcomes, and strengths to be developed. The components of the analysis are necessary for your journey.

i. What you want

ii. Opportunities you can create

iii. What outcomes would create success

iv. Strengths now and strengths to be developed

What you want	Opportunities to create
What outcomes create success	**Strengths to be developed**

Destination 3: Long-Term Goal and Short-Term SMART Goals

Travel this destination when you are in discomfort zone two, Tinkering, and just about to enter zone three, Chaotic Confusion.

Before you hit your third destination, define how you will create goals. The most popular method is based on the SMART acronym. Are you familiar with SMART goals? They are: Specific, Measurable, Attainable, Relevant, and Timely. Makes sense, doesn't it? Your short-term goals will be SMART because a vague goal will get you nowhere fast. But only design your short-term goals as SMART, and let your creative imagination run wild with your long-term goal.

Begin the third destination with stating your long-term goal. The goal does not need to be SMART (at least, not right now). Here is where the journey gets a bit more exciting because the long-term goal should not be something reasonable, predictable, or humdrum. I know what you might be thinking: you will never achieve what you really want. So stating a long-term realistic goal—for example, working in a job with a good salary—is the best you can do. I am yawning when I think about such a long-term goal. How about spicing it up a bit? Try this: maybe your desire is to write a book, but not just a book, but a *New York Times* bestseller and later, your book becomes a movie, and then your own talk show . . . Yes, keep going, this is getting fun! Now I am starting to feel much more excitement. Don't stop, I know you can build on the greatness of your long-term goal until you are almost giddy about the possibilities. With a vivid imagination, there are no limits, just promising possibilities. Don't worry right now about how you will achieve your long-term goal, it's not a concern. Instead, write a goal of an image of your life in five or seven or even ten years from now, even if the goal seems so far out. Remember, you are on a journey of discovery, and you will uncover new perspectives and develop strengths that will change what you do and how you do it.

Go ahead, write down that long-term goal and make it a compelling statement of the future you. Of course, you cannot forget the immediate goals, those short-term goals that are accomplished on your journey of discovery. When you consider the short-term goal, write down as many as you can to help you move inches to the next stage. After you have a good list, prioritize the goals in the order in which you will accomplish each goal. So if you have five short-term goals, what need to be accomplished first? Have you designed each goal to build on the previous one? When you look at your short-term goals do you see a path leading to your long-term goal? Great if you answered yes; however, every short-term goal is a step toward the big vision, even if you cannot see the path clearly.

In other words, a short-term goal is backward movement. To understand the connection between your short-term goals and your long-term goal, place your exciting vision on the endpoint of your journey. Then work backwards to identify what must be accomplished at intervals along the point until you reach the beginning of the point. Those intervals are your short-term goals. Mapping your short-term goals is a great way to keep on track and to feel a great sense of accomplishment knowing that you are moving and it is continuous movement.

Wait, you're not done yet. Writing the goals was the easy part of the journey. What you will do next for each goal is to identify success factors and challenge factors. You will be applying the mental contrasting concept of being optimistic about achieving your vision, yet realistically approaching challenges. Success factors are things you clearly understand to be imperative to achieving the goal. For example, one of my short-term goals was to leave my job of twenty-two years. Since I was not in a place to achieve my long-term goal of leading a nonprofit, I knew I had to break the hold of job security first, so a success factor was to identify a new job in which I could use my skills, yet not be completely unfamiliar or uncomfortable. Another success factor was to get an interview at the company I selected. See how success factors work? They're measurable and help you not only see movement, but *feel* the movement as well. Once you get accustomed to the sensation of movement, you are hooked.

At the same time, although I do not want to put a damper on your energy, I want you to think about challenge factors. These are barriers to achieving your goal. Without including challenges in your short- and long-term goal design, you would be setting yourself up for failure. Facing the fact that limits do exist tells your inner voice you know you have some work to do, and given time, you will find a way to address each challenge. A challenge factor for me to achieve my short-term goal was lack of self-confidence and fear of failure. I could not disregard these challenges because they played a role in moving forward. I had to figure out a way to work on breaking down the challenges, the walls I built around the goal, or else I would resign to a cold, hard fact: my goal could never be achieved.

One last check before you move to the next destination.

- ✓ Is your long-term goal compelling, exciting, and giving you goose bumps to think about the future you?
- ✓ Are your short-term goals specific?
- ✓ Can you define how you will measure them? *Hint: Mapping the goals is a great visual.*
- ✓ Are your short-term goals relevant to moving you closer to your long-term goal?

Finally, did you factor in a timeframe for completion? The last letter in the SMART acronym dictates the pace of progress. The "T" for Timely often creates stress because when you fall behind on your timeframe, you may have a tendency to stop or get out of sync. This is where an accountability partner, a coach, a friend, or a support group can be your best line of defense against frustration. Ready to keep going to your next destination?

Destination 4: Strategy

Travel this destination when you are in discomfort zone three, Chaotic Confusion.

If you reached the fourth destination, you are ready to put everything together. The destinations you have visited gave you fresh insight into who you are, what you want to do, and where you are heading. By now, you have experienced some, maybe quite a few "a-ha" moments: those moments when you are suddenly struck with something that clearly defines you. As though the moment was always present, you did not see anything until the real you began to grow. Capture those "a-ha" moments because they are valuable in developing an approach leading you to create meaningful action steps.

For the destination of strategy, you may want to create a metaphorical basket to place your purpose statement, WOWS analysis, long and short-term goals, success factors, and challenge factors. All of the components of your destination will be combined to design your strategy.

Purpose statement: to guide your thinking

WOWS analysis: to structure your thinking

Long-term goals: to motivate and inspire you

Short-term goals: accomplished quickly to lead to long-term goal

Success factors: lead to goal achievement

Challenge factors: to break down limitations

Strategy design

Before taking action, develop a strategy using previous insightful exercises and what outcomes you want to see. This is important for understanding what approach will be effective. The work accomplished so far has been leading up to the strategy you will design. This destination is where all of your reflective work and your "a-ha" moments are woven into a tangible plan. Ready to design your strategy?

Long-term goals

Begin with restating your long-term goal, where you see yourself in five to seven years. You want to be motivated and inspired every time you review your strategy. Sometimes a long-term goal and maybe even a short-term goal may need some extra motivation so go ahead and include whatever it takes to get you going. For me, when I was traveling the long road to earn my associate degree, bachelor's degree, master's degree, and doctorate, I could visualize the end, walking down the graduation aisle with other students wearing a cap and gown, but what really motivated me was listening to the graduation song, "Pomp and Circumstance." When I graduated with two associate degrees, my mother bought me an autograph dog (those stuffed animals that your friends sign with fabric pens) wearing a cap. When you pressed the foot, the graduation song played. Every time I squeezed the foot of the dog, tears swelled in my eyes, and even when I was dead tired and wanted to quit, just hearing that song made me sit up straight and continue my journey.

What works for you: a quote, a picture, a song, a video? Whatever keeps you motivated and energized—use it.

Short-term goals

Next, restate your SMART short-term goals to be achieved within six months to a year. Use your "Wants" from your WOWS analysis to craft your short-term goals, then prioritize beginning with the most important and design each goal to build upon the previous goal. Identify what you will measure and commit to a timeframe for achieving the goal.

Outcomes for short-term goals

Think about what outcomes must occur for successful goal achievement. Refer to the success factors that you selected to define the outcomes. Decide how you will measure the outcome by using the "What Outcomes Create Success" from your WOWS analysis. Commit to a timeframe for each outcome, and repeat for each goal listed.

Outcome opportunities

Consider what factors must be present for goal outcomes to occur and make a list for each goal. Use your "Opportunities to Create" from your WOWS analysis, and decide how you will measure the factors. Commit to a timeframe for identifying the factors.

Outcome barriers

Although you have considered the challenges when creating your short-term goals, think about what may create barriers to taking action (e.g., weak motivation, not enough experience, too old, low self-esteem) and decide if the challenge is something you can control or not control. Obviously, age is not in your control, but in the strategy design, do not disregard what is not in your control as irrelevant. Instead, any challenge that creates uncontrollable barriers can be addressed from a different vantage point. Even if a challenge seems impossible right now, you will be amazed at what you can do when you see the challenge in a new light. Be sure to use your "Strengths Now and to Be Developed" from your WOWS analysis to address a solution.

Before you move to your next destination, take a few minutes to read your purpose statement. Where did you post your purpose statement? Does every word of it ring true?

Now review your strategy. What great work you have accomplished! Your purpose statement guides your strategy, and you have connected your goals with your WOWS analysis. What have you learned about yourself from this exercise? Ready to travel to the next destination?

Destination 5: Action Plan

Travel to this destination when you are in discomfort zone three, Chaotic Confusion.

Can you believe you are now ready to take action? Because you spent quality time designing your strategy, the action plan is really the easy part. The reason why is because the strategy you designed is clear, concise, and focused on achievement.

Strategy is the music you compose and the action plan is your dancing shoes. You are almost ready to get out on the dance floor and show everyone your smooth moves.

You want the action plan to be detailed; therefore, begin with the goal you have prioritized as most important. It is much easier to work on action with one goal in mind instead of all of them at once. When stating actions, think about what you will do as if you were following a recipe. My grandmother could bake the best plum coffeecake, yet when I asked her for her recipe, she said, "There is no recipe. I just put some flour, eggs, milk, and other ingredients together and bake." It's a real shame her delicious plum coffeecake can never be replicated because she held the recipe in her head. Similarly, don't keep your actions in your head. Write them down, measure them, and commit to a timeline for completion. Most important is that the actions you create are daily actions. They do not have to be grandiose—making a phone call, sending an email, journaling, reading a book, attending a webinar—almost anything you do can be aligned to your goal. Plan your action, document what you have done, and in a short time, you will discover how quickly and effectively you are moving. A point to remember is, as you get into the rhythm of structured action, new opportunities will suddenly appear and you will be ready for the challenge. You will be poised to move because you are not starting from a dead stop, similar to Serena Williams, tennis pro, bouncing on the balls of her feet, ready to spring into action, muscles flexed: momentum awaiting direction.

Given that you only one more destination to go on your journey of discovery, do not think about it as a final destination. Your journey is a lifelong discovery, and with each destination you stop and enjoy, you leave with a wealth of knowledge, a deep appreciation for who you are, and a clear understanding of your purpose.

Destination 6: Checkpoint

Travel this destination when you are in discomfort zone four, Breathing.

Sometimes, even the best plans do not always work out as designed. Your strategy and action may be clear, concise, focused, and attainable, yet you may not be reaching the outcome you anticipated. For this reason, your sixth destination will give you an opportunity to evaluate your progress, acknowledge your accomplishments, and make necessary adjustments to your strategy or to your action plan. This destination is a resting place, a time to relax for a minute, knowing your journey of discovery is easing the pain of discomfort. As you get ready to continue, look back and see how far you have traveled from the moment you decided something was missing, and you set out to create a life with greater meaning and purpose. The destination does not need to be a straight path. Sometimes, the detours in your life offer the best discoveries. Go ahead and look. I think you will be astonished at what you see.

You may be wondering if a destination is missing. How about the destination for discomfort zone five, Victorious? Your journey of discovery really has many destinations; so many, in fact, it would be impossible to even try to list their variety. Your itinerary is designed to propel you into action and keep you moving. Once you are on your way, the destination for discomfort zone five is waiting for your arrival. You will know when you reach it by the smile on your face, the overwhelming sense of accomplishment, and a true feeling of purpose and meaning in your work. I can see it already, so will you.

9 Success Enablers

Life can be a journey toward purpose and meaning—if you ask the right questions.
—Marina Keegan

Recall the winding road metaphor from Chapter Two? Where you're driving along a beautiful country road enjoying the scenery without a care in the world until suddenly fog, rocks, and darkness engulf the road, and you are in state of panic because you cannot move forward and are unable to turn back? It's a really scary place to be, especially without a GPS, a companion, or a cell phone. You realize rather quickly you are stuck, immobile, and hoping something changes real soon. Let me continue the rest of the story where I get to describe a happy ending.

What is that in the distance? A light, a small speck of light? You slowly put pressure on the accelerator. The highest rate of speed you will even chance is about fifteen mph. Your hands are clenched on the wheel, your eyes keep moving from the road to the light as you drive over rocks feeling like boulders and bumps in the road; the light appears to get brighter. You cannot even imagine where the light could be coming from, and you hope this road is nearing an end. As you get closer to the light, you also see a figure, someone holding a lantern. Who could be walking on this road? Where is the figure going? Am I in real danger now? The grip on the wheel tightens as you approach the silhouette and your breathing becomes heavy. Wait, no, it cannot be. Yes, it is: your best friend. A smile and deep sigh of relief overwhelms you, and your anxiety seems to dissolve instantly as you realize you are no longer traveling alone.

Your friend is surprised to see you, too, and smiles back.

"Where am I and what are you doing here?" you ask.

"I walk this path often. While the short stretch of road is hidden in fog, if you keep walking, you will discover the most beautiful, serene, and interesting path. I walk here often, although the first time I strolled here, I wanted to turn back; however, I was happy I kept hiking on the foggy path for just a little bit longer," she replies.

She goes on to say, "Would you like me to ride with you and show you the route? You just have a little ways to go, and when you get there, you'll be amazed. I promise you will not regret driving on the dark, rocky path when you see what lies beyond the fog."

Now, more than likely, even if you did not stumble on your friend walking along, you would have discovered the beautiful path. But the journey would have taken much longer, your anxiety level would have been extremely high, and you would have no one to share your experience of driving on a foggy road to sheer beauty. Being with your friend who knows the path is reassuring, comforting, and provides a sense of relief from a stressful situation.

Similarly, your journey of discovery is a winding road filled with rocks, bumps, and fog. The outcome, when you look past the mist, the anxiety, and the tight grip on the "you of the past," is finding that beautiful place. When you finally arrive, you will realize that the discovery of who you were meant to be occurred because you were able to weather the painful parts, find joy in new experiences, and follow a vision of your ideal life.

While the journey of discovery is really lifelong, the purpose of discovery is to move to the final discomfort stage, Victorious, where discomfort does not exist. Therefore, in addition to developing habits, crafting a purpose statement, identifying long- and short-term goals, developing a strategy, and designing an action plan, there is one more factor essential to reaching the Victorious stage. You must create success enablers to make the journey of discovery come alive, support your actions, and give you a boost to stage five, Victorious, much quicker than anticipated.

Accelerate Your Success Rate

Whenever I recall my success enabler, I think back to a time when I only dreamed about my calling and purpose. For thirty years, I felt like a failure because I did not graduate high school. I continually told myself I was not smart enough to ever consider attending college, and my inner voice kept me informed about what I believed was true. I had so many walls of fear that continued to build and build, until I could not see any hope for change. I always understood the value of never giving up and never giving in, except I took the futile stance that I would never give up feeling like a failure and never give in to the possibility that I had the power to change my life.

Surprisingly, when I was forty-eight years old, something strange happened, and suddenly everything was different. I experienced my first success: passing the GED Math test. Of course, earning my GED stopped the flow of negative thoughts, jolted my behavior, and sparked new life. My long-held beliefs were shattered in one instance and my eyes were opened to new possibilities. While it may be true I could have developed a strategy to continue my success, I doubt I would have had the motivation and determination to reach my goal. Transforming thoughts, words, and actions do not occur with one successful accomplishment; instead, transformation from who you are to who you are meant to be is a lifelong experience of awakening new emotions, inspiring actions that are meaningful, and sensing sheer joy in being you. Because of the first experience with success, my journey of discovery has taught me five of the most important lessons to accelerate goal achievement, both long- and short-term, and I would like to share them with you.

1. **Create a corner of support.** You cannot travel the journey of discovery alone. Well, you can, but it's an uphill battle and it's a slow, tiring, journey. Before I had the itch, the craving to follow my passion, I did not consider asking for help and reflecting on my actions. I now realize two reasons why I could not get up enough courage to reach out. One, I was too embarrassed to admit my failure. I never discussed my lack of education, and when conversations involved class reunions or college adventures, I found a way to either change the subject or excuse myself. No one knew I was a high-school dropout. Second, I perceived asking for help to be a sign of weakness, and heaven knows I had way too many weaknesses without exposing more. Not until the day I walked into College of DuPage during registration to take my final GED exams, including Math, did I learn support was necessary and available. When I finished taking the remaining test and turned in my work, I waited impatiently for the scores. The tester announced I had passed the two tests, Literature and Math, and the entire room—students, instructors, and staff—cheered and clapped. I cried. All of a sudden, everyone I encountered kept encouraging me to continue, keep going, and earn a degree. I am so happy I changed the way I perceived support because early in my educational journey, I can recall two incidents when I threw my hands up and wanted to quit.

In other words, I could not do it any longer; I was tired, frustrated, and feeling like an imposter, trying to pass Business Math and Intro to Computers. At this point, it was impossible to rationalize any longer why I was doing this to myself. I must really have been a sad mess because my family, my mentors, fellow students, and my instructors guided me, gave me words of encouragement, and cheered me to the finish line. I am thankful every day for my support team. In addition, there is another corner of support you must build: a new circle of support.

- **Entering a new circle.** As you move through the stages of discomfort, you will notice a change in your thinking, behavior, and actions. So will your current circle of relationships. That is, where you are now centered may not be a good fit for who you are becoming. I am not suggesting abandoning good, established relationships; just be aware that the natural process of change will alter the circle of relationships for you.

Several years ago, I searched on Facebook for people I knew. I was so excited to find Betty, my best friend all the way through kindergarten, grade school, and the few years I was in high school. I had so few friends when I was growing up that finding one was quite a big deal. Since we lost contact with each other about thirty years ago, we communicated by email a few times and decided to meet for dinner. It had been such a long time, I wasn't sure if I would recognize her. As I entered the restaurant, Betty was waiting in the lobby. We hugged and cried and stood there looking at each other. (I hope she wasn't thinking how old I looked.) During dinner, we talked endlessly about the past, recalling every memorable incident as if we were still in school. Finally, we brought our lives up to date with the present. As she discussed her retirement, gardening, and playing with the grandchildren, I was describing my dissertation, how I was going to develop my business, write a book, and become a professional speaker. Clearly, I no longer belonged in her circle of relationships any more than she belonged in mine. Many years ago, we shared a circle, and since our paths are so different now, we each belong to a new circle, serving a purpose for where we are now.

As you move through the stages of discomfort closer to your calling, find people and groups who are doing work you want to do and enter into their circle. Don't worry; at first, you will feel totally out of place and not comfortable because the people in this new circle are known experts and credible professionals with a wealth of experience. You, on the other hand, may not exactly fit in that category, but want to hang with the crowd anyway. Use your awkwardness and vulnerability to your advantage, given that the people in the new circle are just as curious about you as you are curious about their work. Connect by asking for information and be willing to learn from them. Coffee and conversation is the best approach and creates an environment for support, resource sharing, and golden nuggets of information, just the things you need where you are at now.

When conducting research, you know you're on the right path when you find the same authors writing about a topic over and over again. Similarly, you can measure your change by the people in your circle. If you attend events, workshops, presentations, and you meet the same people, you know you belong to the right circle. The advantage of entering a new circle is the people there know who you are, not who you have been, and the more interaction you have, the greater the feeling of belonging.

2. **Derive power from your strengths, not weaknesses.** I spent most of my life focused on my weakness. I couldn't do math so, I was never able to overcome the weakness. When I changed my focus and devoted all of my attention to my strengths, I soared. Use your strengths and downplay your weaknesses because as you continue to develop your strengths, your weakness will also get a boost. Besides, weaknesses are just undeveloped strengths and you can get around to them after you have achieved your goals.

3. **Challenge your limitations.** Eleanor Roosevelt said it best: "You must do the things you think you cannot do." Break down each of your perceived limitations, push them out of the way and do what you need to do. Ask and challenge yourself, "Why can't I do that?" Answer that question honestly. When you feel you can't go any further, just push a little harder. I guarantee it is an exhilarating feeling producing outstanding results, and every time you push, you become stronger for the next limitation.

- **Design your breakthroughs.** Given that limitations can put a halt to plans that have the ability to move you forward, you need to decide what limitations you want to crush. One of the most interesting ways to approach limitation breakthroughs is by using your "A-ha/Oh-no" Journal described in Breakthrough Exercise 3. In a short time, you will see that you are breaking down perceived limitations, especially those long-held limitations that put the brakes on any attempts to change in the past. Another bonus to breaking down limitations is your inner voice will probably go in a corner and pout because you are taking flight instead of living in fright.

4. **Find your passion and follow it.** The strongest driving force for reaching your goal is passion. When that drives your actions, you have unbelievable energy, unlimited enthusiasm, and purpose beyond goal achievement. You have a calling, a role to play, and a deeper meaning for your life. Within your passion lies your purpose. Follow it, and you will be thoroughly surprised at where it will lead you. Passion and purpose are a winning combination.

5. **Reward yourself.** You deserve it, so go ahead give yourself a reward! Not only for the big wins, but for even the teeny tiny ones. Every feel-good moment deserves a personal acknowledgement—a reward makes the effort you are putting into your journey worthwhile. By far, a reward is one of the strongest motivator to continue the journey, even when you are experiencing frustrations, confusion, and anxiety. It boosts your energy, your confidence, and your enthusiasm and, most importantly, it's especially designed for you. With this intention in mind, understand the reward does not need to be something tangible or expensive. For example, after writing in your "A-ha" column, reward yourself with a day off to do nothing, or after achieving a short-term goal, you could indulge in a hot fudge sundae, whipped cream and cherry optional. (Really though, who can eat a hot fudge sundae without whipped cream and cherry?) Of course, vacations, new shoes, tickets to a game, movie, or concert, dinner at a special restaurant, or anything to make you feel good is all part of the deal. By presenting yourself with a reward, you are actually giving yourself a personal pat on the back for moving in the direction of your dreams, and the journey is a little less tiring.

Success enablers are more than mere action. While you may have many more success enablers serving the same purpose as the important lessons I shared, use every available source to help and guide you and encourage action. At some point, you might meet resistance to change from people who supported you in the past because your change has impact on everyone you encounter. Therefore, the success enablers provide a variety of ways to combat or maintain the wide array of feelings you are experiencing. This is especially true since you may feel stuck, overwhelmed, or discouraged from time to time during your journey of discovery.

Soon, you will reach the Victorious stage, and your success enablers will trigger the movement necessary to get there. Don't fret if you can't seem to get past Chaotic Confusion. More than likely, right now, the "you" of the past will not let it happen and the test is who will conquer. The battle of the two "you"s will continue until you become stronger than who you were. You know there is a light at the end of the tunnel, but cannot see one. It's so frustrating. Take heart: the reason for your frustration is that the light you are seeking at the end of the tunnel does not exist yet. You will need to use a match right now, and every time your match burns to the end, strike another one. Eventually, you will use fewer and fewer matches, and the light you are seeking will come from *you*, not from someone else and not from an artificial source. You will shine bright because the real you will emerge, and when it does, your purpose, your passion, and meaning will carry you into Victorious.

10 Discomfort Is Comfortable

The end of all of our exploring will be to arrive where we started and know the place for the first time.
—T.S. Eliot

Time to take a deep breath and exhale. Do it again and again. Close your eyes, quiet your mind, and sit still for a few minutes. An amazing thing happens when you do that simple exercise: for that one moment in time, you are in the present and the sense of calm you are feeling is real. Maybe it has been a long time since you enjoyed being in the present because you have been focused on your vision, your goal, and breaking down your fears.

Now look back. No, don't turn your head— look back through the lens of your mind and reflect on who you were when you started the journey of discovery and who you are now. Wherever you are, in your stage of discomfort or your "a-ha" moments, stop and breathe. Put aside frustrations, stress, and anxiety and allow your mind to be still.

Slowly, ask yourself:

- What do I see?
- What new discoveries about myself have I gathered?
- What new thoughts have entered my mind?

It's helpful to think back and recall the first moment you got the itch to change. For me, I relive the time again and again, because that lost, yet hopeful feeling is a reminder of my life purpose poking its head out and beckoning me to follow. I know the itch was present for a long time before I took any action. I really tried not to concentrate on it, hoping it would eventually disappear. Without much effort on my part, every morning driving to work, I would envision my life as being much different than the one I was experiencing. Not that I had a clear picture of what I was doing but the vision was more about having freedom to choose my work, my time, and my relationships. The vision was a far cry from how I lived.

Generally speaking, my existence was routine, ordinary, and uneventful. I don't crave drama; in fact, I believe I designed my life to eliminate any drama, not make waves, and live relatively unnoticed, and as long as I continued to act as a responsible mother, wife, employee, and daughter, I *should* (note the word I used) not ask for more. After all, who was I to think I could become anything more, especially since I was a failure, a high school dropout, and an underachiever? Success was for smart, innovative, and extroverted people. I truly believed I did not possess any of those strengths, and as long as I held onto that belief, I was able to tolerate the nagging discomfort I felt. I was comfortable in my discomfort. I kept dismissing the itch as daydreaming and I tried not to fade from reality too many times a day. Of course, you know how well that worked. Rather, I found myself escaping reality quite often.

Today, when I look back, I am grateful for embarking on the path of discovery, scratching my itch, and leaving my comfort zone. The journey of discovery is profound, and the outcome of your travel, creating habits, following an itinerary, and designing success enablers is becoming who you are meant to be. Your passion and your purpose is your calling, and even though it may have been dormant for some time, you have the strength, power, tenacity, and understanding necessary to live life with greater meaning and purpose.

In this book, I have shared not only my personal experience along the journey, but evidence-based practices introduced by experts in the field of change. The most interesting thing about your expedition is that you design your travel to accommodate your stage of discomfort. You align action with where you are going because you're not following a process or cookie-cutter procedure designed for just anyone who desires personal change. Your journey is unique, life-changing, and amazing. What you feel in each stage of discomfort is growing pains, and with every one, you are rewarded with a deeper understanding of who you are. Thank goodness the growing pains do not leave stretch marks. Instead, the marks of breaking down barriers and converting fear to energy are visible in your thoughts, actions, and behavior. And those marks are keepers, for sure.

What Is Different?

If I posed the question, "What is different?" to you now, more than likely you would respond with, "Not much," or, "Nothing." Or maybe your response would be a definite, "I am not in control and I am confused." Sound familiar? The reason for this type of a response is that while embarking on a journey of discovery can be life-altering, your life is moving slowly, and changes are subtle, powerful, and silent. The gradual difference in your thoughts, actions, and perception is not as obvious as, say, changing hair color from mousey brown to a ravaging blonde or redhead. Although you may suddenly be inclined to make outward changes such as a new wardrobe (what a good excuse to shop!) or to test a bolder eye shadow or head out on the open road without a particular destination. Sounds risky and fun.

During your discovery voyage you will want to have new experiences. Your old way of thinking will be challenged, and sudden bursts of joy (yes, even in the Chaotic Confusion stage) will provide the opportunity for you to be daring, audacious, and fearless, even if the leap you take is only a small variation from the ordinary. The fact you felt the urge to move in a new direction is enough to understand something is different—very wonderfully so.

How about new opportunities? It's not chance or luck that suddenly they seemingly fall from the sky: you have invited them into your life. The vision you hold, the calling you feel, and the passions stirring your soul exist for a purpose. Without intentional action, the energy you generate as you move by inches toward your goal attracts what you need at just the right moment. You may doubt that openings will materialize before your eyes, when you've never had any good opportunities ever appear without hard work.

Henriette Anne Klauser, PhD, author of *Write it Down, Make it Happen: Knowing What You Want and Getting It* (Fireside Books, 2001), explains how the brain reacts when you write down a goal. The act of penning what you want (purpose statement, WOWS analysis) alerts your brain, specifically the reticular activating system (RAS) that new data is coming through. As the brain filters the information and separates the unimportant from the most important, what you want has been transmitted directly to the brain as high importance. Therefore, your brain is set on maximum alert for opportunities, and in a way, it begins to send "text messages" to you to move in the direction of an opportunity, leading you closer and closer to your goal.

However, let me clarify one thing about the brain and opportunities. You see, your brain can only send alerts to you when you have a clear vision, a strong desire, and you're really committed to achieving your dream—not just a vague idea of what you want but a clear picture, a colorful vision with all the bells and whistles, and a strong, somewhat nagging desire to achieve the goal sooner rather than later. When your vision is vague, your brain's filter of really good stuff and not-so-good stuff is weak; therefore, the data entering your brain is categorized as unimportant, and you will get around to it later, much later. To get your brain wired for high importance, speak confidently, focus your actions, and behave as if you have reached your goal. In other words, it is time for you to tell a new story.

A New Story, a New You

What man thinks of himself, that is which determines, or rather indicates, his fate.
—Henry David Thoreau

Your story, your life, got you where you are today. For all outward appearances, it may be quite impressive, and to many people, you are successful. But the story that has the most impact on you is the story you tell yourself. What I mean is there are two separate stories of your life: the visible story is about your childhood, your family, your career, and what you share with others, and the other story is invisible to everyone but you. You have a tendency to repeat it over and over again in your mind until every word becomes what you believe as the truth, regardless of how different the invisible story is from the visible one. I would suppose your inner voice shares some of the credit for the story you tell yourself and as you progress through the stages of discomfort, adding many exciting twists and turns to the plot.

As much as I would like to agree with what others believed, my visible story was that I had a successful banking career, I was well-educated, and was happy and content with my life. The fact of the matter was my invisible story was quite different than the one portrayed to everyone. The one I told myself for over thirty years was that I was a high-school dropout, a failure, an underachiever, and really not intelligent. I made bad choices, and was totally embarrassed about my past. Regardless of what was occurring in my life—the fact that my invisible story directed my thoughts and behavior—I was never really comfortable and often felt like an imposter. Because most of my life hinged on my weaknesses and things I could not do or not do well at all, my invisible story was told from a negative perspective. But at the turning point, a fateful moment in time, when I finally conquered one of my greatest fears: passing the GED math test, my invisible story changed, and for once, my inner voice was speechless. In that moment of silence, I heard a new voice. It was my voice telling me that I DID IT! My story changed from failure to victory. Suddenly, I was seeing everything with new eyes as I emerged through the foggy lens of doubt, fear, and distrust.

Given you are embarking on a journey of discovery, what story do you tell yourself? Are the words of your invisible story self-defeating or self-motivating? How often is your story repeated in your mind? What do you think will be the moment, your turning point? Every action, movement, or "a-ha" moment has the potential to alter your story, your belief about yourself. Open your mind and your heart, and let the "you" that has been hidden away for so long emerge, so the turning point is really an awakening to the unbelievable possibilities lying ahead. When your visible story and your invisible story are one and the same, aligned with your goals, your purpose, and your passion, you will understand the moment that turned your life from who you thought you were to who you are meant to be.

When I Was at My Best

Several years ago, one of the exercises I was required to complete in my coaching coursework was to write about "when I was at my best." At the time, I didn't put much thought to the exercise since I did not need to submit the paper for a grade. However, I was expected to be able to discuss how I felt after I wrote the paper and how knowing when I was at my best would help me discover a new approach to reaching my goal. Needless to say, I dismissed the entire episode as somewhat irrelevant and I set the paper aside. I didn't even read it aloud after I completed the assignment or share my experience with the other coaching students. Recently, I was thumbing through a stack of papers (I always seem to be looking for something), and I came across the past assignment and read the paper out loud. I stopped for a minute after reading, and suddenly realized how my life story, the story I told myself over and over again, really created limitations for the best of me to shine. Here is what I wrote.

> For most of my life, my best was based on the approval rating of my family, my teachers, my employer, or my friends. My best was directed at maintaining a consistent satisfaction level with everyone, regardless of their connection to me. I never thought about my actions or my behavior because I followed what other people wanted me to do. I believed that I was at my best when I did not

create any conflict, when I placed other people's needs before my needs, and when I accepted other people's opinion as fact without question. In other words, I was at my best when everyone I encountered was happy. My best was not measured by my strengths, my passion, or my needs. Instead, my best was measured by the reaction of the people in my life.

While I was content with my best, whatever best looked like, at age 48, I suddenly found myself questioning my purpose in life. I was not sure if I was experiencing a midlife crisis but the feeling was strong enough to make me think about new possibilities. Some may say that what I was feeling was a natural reaction to the biological process of aging. In any case, my desire to make drastic changes to my life began a twelve-year life-changing journey that continues to define who I am as a person, not as a mother, sister, wife, employee, or student, but exposing the real me. Of course, for me, my journey was life-changing. For others, who I strived to keep happy most of my life, my behavior was radical, unrecognizable, and unnerving. Needless to say, self-discovery was painful, chaotic, and discomforting.

However, life has become much calmer. I can now reflect back on my earlier years, as if I were watching a movie, a drama with a touch of humor, and realize I was at my best whenever I was presented with a challenge, had enough confidence in my ability to meet the challenge, and had support to guide me. In addition, my best would shine when I had the latitude to be creative and a specific timeline for achieving my objectives. In particular, I was at my best when I was an adult student in college because I continually felt challenged, I was applying my talents and strengths like never before, and I received excellent feedback that helped me to improve my communication with others. I was critically thinking about what I was hearing, seeing, and feeling.

It may appear that I was at my best at different seasons of my life. That is, if I felt at my best, I was at my best. Because I have spent so much time immersed in self-discovery, I know now that my best is yet to come. The real me is shining through the clouds of my past, and although my past has provided the framework for who I am, I am just beginning to understand my unique strengths, my passion, and my purpose for existing in this world. My previous achievements, regardless how large or small, only serve as a barometer of what is yet to come when I am fully engaged in being at my best all of the time.

When are you at your best? I would venture to say your best has appeared many times in your journey, yet you may not have fully understood your best during stages of discomfort: Exploration, Tinkering, Chaotic Confusion, or Breathing. Maybe your best appeared in Victorious stage; what do you think? Your best, whatever best is to you, empowers your actions, your thoughts, and the story you tell yourself and tell others. When you are at your best, your story is definitely self-motivating, inspiring, and filled with energy and passion.

> *We will discover the nature of our particular genius when we stop trying to conform to our own or to other people's model, learn to be ourselves, and allow our natural channel to open.*
> **—Shakti Gawain**

What's Next?

As you continue your journey to the final stage, just imagine the feeling when you get to the end of the road, and you are victorious. After all you have endured, you can finally shout to the world, "I DID IT"! You will breathe easier, relax a bit, and sleep more soundly than you have done in a long time. Linger on that thought a while and *know* that you will arrive.

While you linger, let me share the really exciting part of reaching the end of your journey. As you stand victorious, basking in the glow of what you have accomplished, something interesting is happening. Guess what? The itch comes back. Maybe not immediately (well, pretty close), and you find yourself smack dab in the Exploration stage again. I know what you're thinking: "No, cannot be, I won't let that happen." Hold on, this time you will welcome the discomfort, all of the stages. The reason the cycle begins again is because you have created a path of purpose, meaning, and passion and who you are meant to be is just beginning to tap into all of your dreams and possibilities. Your best, like mine, is still evolving, and there is so many more untapped opportunities awaiting you.

Furthermore, all of the life lessons, reflections, and breaking down of limitations and fears you have experienced during your journey of discovery have given you strength, courage, and tenacity to reach even higher, so continuing the journey from here on out will be much different. That is, the discomfort you feel in each stage will not be prolonged, and you will move quite seamlessly through the stages, all the while grasping at the opportunities lining the trail to your next goal.

In other words, the very first step you took, maybe so long ago, set the wheels in motion for you to follow your calling, design an ideal life, and choose work that matters. The pain of change was not in vain. In your discomfort, you gained wisdom, learned valuable lessons, met challenges head on, conquered your fear of leaving your illusionary comfort zone, and drove through the fog to discover the most beautiful place where the real you resides.

There is no stopping now—you are on your way.

Can you hear the crowd cheering you on? The celebration is getting louder and happier. Keep running toward the finish line of who you are meant to be and know that the most interesting discovery on your journey was YOU.

It is good to have an end to journey toward; but it is the journey that matters in the end.
—Ursula K. Le Guin

The Journey of Discovery

Break Down the Brick Walls of Fear

1. Fear of the unknown
2. Fear of failure
3. Fear of abandonment
4. Fear of what others will think
5. Fear of success

Move Through Discomfort Stages

1. Exploration
2. Tinkering
3. Chaotic Confusion
4. Breathing
5. Victorious

Develop Movement Habits

1. Create urgency
2. Choose your move
3. Move by inches, not feet
4. Amplify your self-awareness
5. Use your vision as your guide

Travel the Roads of Destination

1. Purpose statement
2. WOWS analysis
3. Long/short term goal
4. Strategy
5. Action plan
6. Checkpoint

Heighten Your Success Enablers

1. Create a corner of support/enter a new circle

2. Derive power from your strengths, not weaknesses

3. Challenge your limitations/design your breakthrough

4. Find your passion and follow it

5. Reward yourself.

The Journey of Discovery of YOU

Arrive!

About the Author

Susan Neustrom, Ed.D. is a life and leadership coach, professional speaker, consultant, and adjunct professor at National Louis University in the College of Professional Studies and Advancement, at Benedictine University in the undergraduate writing program, and at Argosy University in the Graduate School of Management and Business. Susan has over twenty-five years of experience in leadership positions as Executive Director of a nonprofit, delivering educational programs to incarcerated men and women in the county jail, as Director of Human Resources for a nonprofit agency, working with adults with development disabilities, and as Assistant Vice President for a community bank. She holds an Ed.D. in Organizational Leadership from Argosy University, a M.A. in Organizational Leadership with a training and development concentration from Lewis University, and a B.S. in Management from National Louis University. Susan has served on the Board of Directors for the Wheaton Chamber of Commerce, Family Shelter Service, The American Cancer Society, as a member of the National Louis University Adjunct Council, and as a pro bono HR consultant and coach for Taproot Foundation.

Although her career in banking spanned twenty-two years, advancing from entry level to assistant vice president, she deeply desired to follow her calling and transition to a career in human services to work with people who experience barriers to success. Her passion stemmed from her many years of volunteer work, beginning when she was just fifteen, helping those who were homeless, victims of domestic violence, experiencing crisis pregnancy, unemployed, seniors on a fixed income, and suffering from cancer. But to change her vision to reality, she had to face her greatest fear of failure, leave her comfort zone, and make a life-changing decision. Susan dropped out of high school at age sixteen, yet at age forty-eight, over thirty years after leaving school, she decided to pursue a formal education from GED to Doctorate. Her personal journey of discovery is motivating and inspiring helping many people leave their comfort zone and accomplish great things.

As a result of her life-changing experience, her work and her passion for helping others, Susan is a keynote speaker, presenter, and facilitator at many universities, conferences, and organizations. Her workshops are highly interactive and focus on leaving your comfort zone, leading change, and discovering meaning and purpose.

Susan lives in Woodridge, IL with her husband, two dogs, and a cat. She has two children, a son and daughter, two granddaughters, and two great-granddaughters. She is a lifelong Beatle fan and believes that her motivation to pursue her dream was really inspired by the Beatles' ongoing determination to break down limitations, see beyond the "what is," and never let go of their vision.

She admits that, even to this day, she still experiences bouts of Beatlemania every time she hears a Beatle song.

Really would like to hear from you...

As you travel on your Journey of Discovery, you will experience "a-ha" moments and face some "oh-no" moments through various stages of discomfort. Please share those moments with me. I would really like to hear about your experience, celebrate your success, and applaud your determination, persistence, and your accomplishments. Please contact me at: susan@susanneustrom. com to share your story.

Having a partner and additional support on your Journey of Discovery enhances your experience and increases your breakthrough moments. I can help you design a comfort zone with a door to exit and enter. Learn more about one-on-one coaching or group coaching at www.susanneustrom.com.

Want a few more resources and tools for your Journey of Discovery? Visit The Comfort Zone Illusion website at www. thecomfortzoneillusion.com.

Looking for a speaker at your next event? Contact me at media@susanneustrom.com.

Comfort Zone workshops

Presentations

Keynote

Let's connect on social media...

Follow me on Twitter: http://twitter.com/SusanNeustrom

Like me on Facebook: http://www.facebook.com/susan.neustrom

Connect with me on LinkedIn: http://www.linkedin.com/in/susanneustrom

Leaving your comfort zone is not so hard after all!

CPSIA information can be obtained at www.ICGtesting.com
Printed in the USA
BVOW06s1108110116

432402BV00001B/22/P